Full Circle

The Rise, Fall and Rise of Horse Racing in Chelmsford

David Dunford

Essex Hundred Publications

Essex Hundred Publications
www.essex100.com ask@essex100.com

FULL CIRCLE
David Dunford

British library cataloguing in Publication Data,
A catalogue record for this book is available from
The British Library.
ISBN 9780993108358
Typeset by Hutchins Creative Limited
Printed by 4edge Publishing
22 Eldon Way
Eldon Way Industrial Estate
Hockley Essex SS5 4AD

This book is dedicated to my wife, Anne, for her unfailing support.

Acknowledgements

This book would not have seen the light of day without the enthusiastic help of many people. My grateful thanks are due to:-

Wendy Cummin and the late Ted Hawkins of Galleywood Heritage Centre who have done so much to preserve the history of Galleywood Racecourse. Without their assistance and unrestricted access to their archives this book would not have been possible.

Megan Rose Photography for allowing us to use her brilliant action pictures of Chelmsford City Racecourse and particularly Racecourse Manager Fraser Garrity for his cooperation and a fascinating tour of the new facilities.

The staff of the Albert Sloman Library at Essex University who tracked down obscure books at other libraries around the country. The staff at Essex Record Office who helped me find documents and photographs in their extraordinary archive.

Dr Amanda Wilkinson of the University of Essex who supervised the MA dissertation on which this book is based. Dr Marie-Paule Powell, Professor Emeritus University of Toronto, for her comments and meticulous proof reading.

David Dunford

Contents

Full gallop past St Michael's Church in the 1920s

Illustrations

Unless specified below, images supplied by the author or from the Essex Hundred Collection

Cover back and front: Megan Rose Photography and Galleywood Heritage Centre Archives

Period newspaper clippings courtesy of British Newspaper online archive and Essex Libraries.

The finishing post at Galleywood in 1920

Tryster (far side), ridden by Adam Kirby, who won the first race at the new Chelmsford City Racecourse on 11th Jan 2015. He went on to win a £40,000 race at Chelmsford in September that year and was the champion all-weather horse of 2015.

Megan Rose Photography
:Equine:Commercial:Weddings:Photoshoots:

meganrosephoto@gmail.com   07584200553   www.meganrosephotography.co.uk

Introduction

Step back 200 years and the most eagerly awaited highlights of the social calendar were the local horse race meetings. They were so popular that nearly a dozen towns and villages in Essex held them and they drew thousands of spectators. But by far the most successful of these were Chelmsford Races held on Galleywood Common just three miles from the town centre. So popular were they that as early as the 1770s the local gentry raised money for a permanent grandstand where they could view the races safely isolated from the lower classes.

The races had an attraction for everyone across the great social divide – not just the racing itself but also the many social events that went on in conjunction with it. Horse racing in the late eighteenth and early nineteenth centuries was very different to the sport we know today. Organised gambling was unknown and betting was largely confined to the upper classes. Horses were older since they had to be walked between meetings and young ones couldn't stand the strain. Fields were small – often no more than a dozen horses were involved in a three-day meeting. The lack of entries was made up for by running races in as many as three heats, usually of three or four miles. Because of the number of heats and the length of the races, horses often began at a trot then moved into a canter and only began to gallop over the last mile or so. So it was not surprising that race meetings evolved other attractions.

For the aristocracy and the elite they were a way of displaying their wealth and underlining their social status; for the few who felt they could break out of the straightjacket of a rigid class structure they provided the opportunity to move up the social ladder by mixing with their 'betters'. For the great mass of working people, far too poor to ever attend the great social events, the races themselves offered a good day out and the chance to meet friends in a carnival atmosphere. The racecourse was crammed with sideshows – small theatres, boxing booths, jugglers, acrobats, card sharps and many beer tents. With a good number of the spectators the worse for wear, the races were also a popular target for the criminal minority. A meeting in July 1833 led to enough people being hauled into court to fill an entire column in the *Chelmsford Chronicle.*

But this spectacular social occasion didn't last. A century of technological and social developments changed the nature of Chelmsford Races to such a degree that they simply couldn't survive in the twentieth century. Change came slowly at first. In the late eighteenth and early nineteenth centuries cockfighting was an important element of Chelmsford Race meetings. They were often held at the Saracen's Head in the town centre as well as on the course and attracted huge prize money. But as people began to become concerned about animal welfare cockfighting died out – it was last recorded in Chelmsford in 1833.

The catalyst for the biggest change in horse racing came with the arrival of the railway in Chelmsford in 1842. It meant spectators began to arrive from a wide area and the races became less important as a major local social event. The railways also changed the nature of racing itself; horses could be transported quickly and, crucially, it meant young horses could be raced. This in turn led to a shortening of races and the introduction of professional jockeys – younger horses in shorter races were given lighter weights to carry and these were weights to which no portly amateur gentleman jockey of the time would think of reducing.

As the nineteenth century progressed other social and commercial changes came into play. The aristocracy which had done so much to support racing in Chelmsford began to lose power and influence. Other leisure activities began to flourish in the town.

Chelmsford Races also lost spectators to the newly arrived enclosed racecourses, the first of which opened at Sandown Park in 1875. Although these courses charged a general admission fee and not just for the grandstand as at Chelmsford, they became immediately successful. They offered better facilities, most had their own railway station and offered high class racing. Flat racing at Chelmsford came to an end around 1880 when the Jockey Club ruled that the minimum prize money should be £300 a day. The course was converted to steeplechasing but Chelmsford Races continued a slow decline and by 1935 could no longer survive.

The history of Chelmsford Races might have ended in the dark days of the 1930s had it not been for a local entrepreneur, John Holmes. In 1997 he bought the old Essex Showground at Great Leighs, five miles to the north of Chelmsford. A £30 million all-weather racecourse was built in 2008 and marked the return of racing to Chelmsford for the first time in more than 70 years. Sadly, the venture faltered and the course went into administration in 2009. Finally a syndicate headed by Fred Done, owner of the Betfred bookmaking chain, rode to the rescue. In its first year (2015), the newly-named Chelmsford City Racecourse held nearly 60 meetings. It also began hosting other events such as concerts, comedy and murder mystery nights – social events that echo those associated with horse racing in Chelmsford 200 years ago.

The start at Chelmsford Races c1930

Part I

Chelmsford Races – A Long History

Horse Racing and the 'Dullest Place on Earth'

At the end of the eighteenth and beginning of the nineteenth centuries horse races were the highlight of the entertainment calendar in many towns across England. Their attraction lay not just in the races themselves but also in the opportunities they afforded for a wide range of other activities both on and off the course which appealed across all social classes.

Race meetings were so popular in the latter part of the eighteenth century that an act designed to stop their unrestricted growth was passed by Parliament. This demanded a prize of at least £50 for each race but had little practical effect and in the early nineteenth century virtually every town of any size in England had its own racecourse. In Essex alone, race meetings are known to have been held in Brentwood, Maldon, Southminster, Braintree, Colchester, Witham, Coggeshall, Tiptree, Epping and Chelmsford, which for a time in the middle of the nineteenth century had two, with courses at Galleywood and Writtle. Even the tiny village of Wennington near the Thames on the Rainham marshes had a race meeting every summer.

They were all extremely popular with races at Epping in 1838 reported to have attracted between four and five thousand people with a similar number put at a meeting in Coggeshall ten years later. But despite the widespread competition, Chelmsford Races, held on Galleywood Common, were by far the most successful. This may have been in part because they were the only ones in Essex to boast royal patronage, having been awarded the annual Queen Charlotte's Plate, worth one hundred guineas, by George III.

Early newspaper advertisement for Chelmsford Races from The Ipswich Journal May 1768.

In the early nineteenth century they were seen as preeminent in the county and the ones to which other towns and villages aspired.

A reporter wrote of Coggeshall Races, for example, '...Old Galleywood must look after its laurels or they will be snatched away...' Wennington races in 1833 were said to have gained much celebrity and had that year 'not fallen off in attraction. They may now vie in interest, sport and company, with any races in the county ... Galleywood, it must be confessed, has in Wennington, found a powerful rival.'

A few years earlier spectators had described Galleywood as 'equal to any race ground in the country' and the course was so successful that it had permanent grandstands, the first of which was erected as early as 1770. But despite the massive popularity of horse races throughout the county, by the early years of the twentieth century only those at Chelmsford remained and by 1935 even they had gone.

Although there is no evidence of horse racing in Chelmsford before 1759, the town was clearly thriving and prosperous well before this. Nearly a century earlier it was visited by Cosmo de Medici, the Grand Duke of Tuscany, as part of a tour through England. He was accompanied by Count Lorenzo Magalotti who described how 'his highness took a walk through the town, which from its population and wealth, ranks among the principal ones in Essex, in the centre of which it stands.'

Daniel Defoe remarked of Chelmsford in 1724 that it was 'full of good inns and chiefly maintained by the excessive multitude of carriers and passengers which are constantly passing this way to London with droves of cattle, provisions and manufactures...' He also noted that it was 'observable that in this part of the country there are several very considerable estates purchased and now enjoyed by citizens of London, merchants and tradesmen ... I mention this to observe how the present increase of wealth in the city of London spreads itself into the country, and plants families and fortunes, who in another age will equal the families of the ancient gentry, who perhaps were bought out.'

This prosperity was reflected by a large amount of redevelopment during the eighteenth century which continued to the end of the century despite the outbreak of war against France in 1793. In 1795 one prominent citizen, Thomas Berney Bramston, wrote:- 'There really seems to be a considerable rage for building about the town of Chelmsford even at this time, and this is very likely to increase whenever we have peace.' The population rose from an estimated 2,700 in 1766 to 3,755 by the turn of the century. It was against this background of prosperity and development that Chelmsford Races were established. However, not everyone had a favourable opinion of the town and Charles Dickens later described it as 'the dullest and most stupid spot on the face of the earth'. He found there was nothing to look at 'except two immense prisons large enough to hold all the inhabitants of the county' (see page 71). The town continued to expand during the nineteenth century and the 1851 census put its population at just under 7,800 which by 1901 had risen to 12,600. However, until the latter part of the century it remained above all a market town little changed from the way Defoe saw it in 1724. As late as 1889-90 the Essex Business Review noted:- 'Chelmsford is ... chiefly known as an important agricultural centre; while the industries of the place are almost entirely such as to have a more or less direct bearing on farming'

However, the foundations of a change to an industrial centre had been laid as early as 1843 when Frederick Greenwood established Coleman and Moreton which, in addition to making agricultural machinery, manufactured steam engines and castings for bridges as well as manhole covers. In the middle of the century Fell Christy opened a business supplying machinery for wind and water mills as well as agricultural machinery and by 1883 this had developed into an electrical and engineering works. But it was not until the last quarter of the nineteenth century that industries began to grow up which had, for the first time, no direct connection with the town's agricultural past. In 1878 Colonel Rookes Crompton founded Crompton and Company Electrical Engineers which was to become one of the most important manufacturers of electrical equipment in Britain. It later became Crompton Parkinson. The Hoffman Manufacturing Company opened at the turn of the century to manufacture ball bearings and became a major employer. The third new type of industrial business to open around this time was Marconi's Wireless Telegraph Company which established the world's first radio factory in Hall Street in 1899.

The administrative importance of the town also grew during this period, although it had been recognised as the county town since the thirteenth century. In 1888 it was incorporated as a borough, in 1889 Essex County Council set up its offices in Duke Street and in 1908 it became the cathedral town of a new diocese. The town continued to grow throughout the early years of the twentieth century and during the Second World War Chelmsford was an important centre of light engineering. As such it became a target for German attacks both by aircraft and rocket. In December 1944 a V2 rocket fell on Henry Road near the Hoffman ball bearing factory and not far from the Marconi factory which had moved to New Street before the First World War. Thirty-nine people were killed and 138 injured, many seriously. A night bombing raid in May 1943 hit the town centre, Moulsham and Springfield and left 50 dead and a thousand people homeless.

Towards the end of the twentieth century the nature of Chelmsford changed beyond recognition. The three major factories disappeared one after another. Marconi's defence division, which included the Chelmsford works, was taken over by British Aerospace in 1999. The New Street factory finally closed in 2008 bringing to an end Marconi's century-long association with the town. In 1922 the world's first regular wireless broadcasts had begun from what was little more than a wooden hut at Writtle under the call sign '2MT'. Today Chelmsford describes itself as 'the birthplace of radio'.

In 1969 Crompton Parkinson was downsized and operations moved elsewhere after a takeover by Hawker Siddley. The Writtle Road factory was acquired by Marconi as a base for the newly formed Radar Systems division. It, too, declined and closed in 1992. Most of the site is now a housing estate.

Hoffman – Britain's first ball bearing factory – and once Chelmsford's main employer with 7,500 personnel became Ransome Hoffman Pollard in 1969. It was wound down during the 1980s and closed for good in December 1989. Most of the factory was demolished and the site is now occupied by the Rivermead Campus of Anglia Ruskin University.

As Chelmsford's position as an industrial centre declined so did its other traditional role as a market town. With widespread re-development, the weekly livestock market moved from the town centre to a site in Victoria Road in 1963. It later moved out of the town completely to a site at Springfield before finally closing in 1999.

The character of the town was changed for ever in the late 1960s with the destruction of the Corn Exchange in Tindal Square and the demolition of much of the ancient nearby Tindal Street to make way for the High Chelmer shopping centre which opened in 1972. Two decades later it was joined by the Meadows precinct which opened on to the by now pedestrianised High Street.

In 1954 the architectural historian, Sir Nikolaus Pevsner said of Chelmsford:- 'A walk through the town does not afford much excitement. But it is pleasant, because the centre has remained singularly unaffected by the coarser and louder forms of commercialisation.' It is unlikely his opinion would be the same today.

After the war the local council set about a programme of house building with a number of new housing estates. In the 1980s and 90s there was extensive development of private estates.

In 2012 a long-running campaign finally bore fruit and the town was awarded city status. Today the population is put at around 170,000. Latest estimates suggest more than 27,000 of them are over the age of 65 – around 16 per cent of the total population.

Although this modern view of the High Street is recognisably similar to that in the nineteenth century (see page 57),
the character of Chelmsford has changed beyond recognition.

Racing at Galleywood

Chelmsford Races were run over common land in the village of Galleywood some three miles from Chelmsford town centre and survived for at least one hundred and seventy years until the final meeting in 1935.

Much of the racecourse still exists. Although a small area was taken for a new Chelmsford bypass in the 1980s, the remainder is still clearly visible. Railings are regularly maintained by the local authority and although the grandstand is long gone, some of the brick ancillary buildings are still in use – one notably as the village heritage centre. The racecourse was unique since with the building of St Michael and All Angels' in the early 1870s it became the only course in the country to encircle a church. Although local legend has it that races at Galleywood date back to the time of Charles I, the first recorded reference can be found in The Ipswich Journal in February 1761 in the form of an advertisement for a horse called Solon which was standing at stud for one day at premises in Colchester having previously won the 'Four-year-old plate at Chelmsford in the year 1759.'

Each year from 1760 Queen Charlotte's Plate, originally sponsored by George III and worth a hundred guineas was raced for by four-year-old fillies over the best of three two-mile heats. (This plate had been awarded to commemorate a visit to the town by Queen Charlotte as she journeyed from Harwich to London.) Other early races included the Gentlemen's Plate worth 50 guineas, which was sponsored by the local nobility and gentry, and the Town Plate, also worth 50 guineas, which was sponsored by Chelmsford residents. A rare surviving example of the race accounts show that in 1814 the town council donated fifteen guineas towards this race.

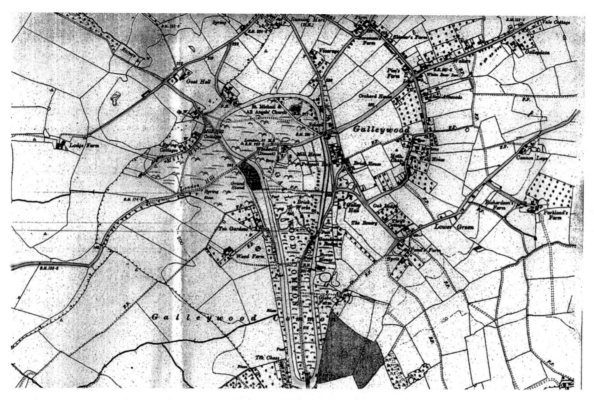

Map showing the racecourse (outlined in green) and the village of Galleywood in 1898. The southern tip of the course is now junction 16 of the A12 bypass.

As the races became more established the elite who ran them decided they should take action to make themselves more comfortable and *The Ipswich Journal* reported in July 1770:-

'At these races the noblemen, gentlemen &c entered into a resolution of erecting a perpetual stand upon the race ground for their accommodation.'

In addition to the degree of comfort they provided, grandstands also provided a source of prize money through a subscription charge; they also added a degree of permanence to the course. In addition, they were a means of social exclusion since only the wealthy could afford the subscription. Although no financial records survive from this period it is known that the race stewards in 1814 subscribed ten guineas each to the races so it is likely the general subscription which allowed access to the stand would have been around this level, equivalent to more than £750 today. By comparison, figures from the Essex Record Office suggest a farm labourer in the county at this time had an annual income of little more than twice that amount. It may be that the sense of permanence given by the stand and the replacements built in subsequent years assisted Chelmsford Races survive longer than most town races and become, during the nineteenth century, some of the most successful. In 1839, when 92 per cent of town courses were holding just one meeting a year, Chelmsford had three.

By 1869 Chelmsford was still holding three meetings a year while 94 per cent of courses held one or two. Only four courses, among them Newmarket, had more annual meetings than Chelmsford during this period. Up to the middle of the nineteenth century a wide range of other activities took place in conjunction with race meetings in Chelmsford itself. These included theatrical performances, balls and dinners. Until the early part of the century cockfighting was also an important element of the race meetings. The heyday of horse racing at Galleywood came in the 1860s when Admiral Henry Rous, who was the senior steward of the Jockey Club, was appointed to oversee meetings. The admiral had his own private grandstand built nearby and, as will be seen later, was a key player in changes which affected the relationship between the races and the town.

The Chelmsford Race Stand Company built a new grandstand in 1863 with a number of rooms plus outbuildings and accommodation. By the end of the 1860s the *Chelmsford Chronicle* reported improvements were complete with 'several of the leading supporters of the turf expressing their congratulations and asserting that nowhere could better accommodation be found ...'

Despite this, the course began a period of slow decline in the 1870s and in 1876 the Chelmsford Chronicle reported that the number of spectators was dwindling with 'the company ... not as numerous as we used to see in days of yore'. The report added:- 'We heard on the stand that the meeting has been held at a loss during the past few years, and the hint was thrown out that ... the races which have recently been reduced from two to one meeting in the year, will be further reduced to a single day's meeting.'

However, the races were still attracting the top jockeys of the day. Among them was Fred Archer whose tragic fate was apparently foretold at Galleywood. In the view of many experts Archer was the greatest jockey ever. He was born in Cheltenham in 1857, the fourth of five children of the National Hunt Jockey, William Archer, who won the 1858 Grand National.

The original grandstand was built in the 1770s, a new one was completed in 1863. This photograph dates from 1914

It soon became apparent that young Fred had a gift for horsemanship and by the age of eight he was riding in local pony races and with the Cotswold Foxhounds. So outstanding was his talent that his father arranged for him to be apprenticed at the age of eleven to a leading trainer at Newmarket. He rode his first race at the age of 14 and his first major win was in the 1872 Cesarewitch. Two years later he became champion jockey at the age of just 17. Archer retained the title for 13 consecutive years until 1886, riding 2,748 winners from 8,084 starts. In 1885 he rode 246 winners, a record that wasn't broken until Gordon Richards' 1933 season. He won the Epsom Derby five times and a total of 21 classic races.

In 1879 the *Essex Chronicle* described a win for Archer at Galleywood riding the favourite, Howdie, in The Boreham Welter Stakes:-

'Upon coming into the straight Bloomfield was leading, with Princess Mathilde nearly level just inside the opposite rails, but upon reaching the hill Archer gradually brought Howdie up, and giving her her head at the finish, came up an easy winner by three quarters of a length.'

At that time jockeys were allowed to bet and Archer was a compulsive gambler but despite the temptations, his honesty was

Fred Archer as seen by Vanity Fair magazine in 1881

never in question and the desire to win was paramount. Indeed, he acquired the nickname 'The Tin Man' because he always went for the prize or 'the tin' as it was known. He was said to have ridden some of his best races against horses he had backed. However, Archer's massive success was bought at a huge price. He had one major problem – his weight. Although he easily made the weight of 5 stone 7lb when he won the Cesarewitch as a teenager as an adult he grew to 5' 9'', exceptionally tall for a jockey. As a result he existed on little food combined with regular laxatives. Inevitably his health suffered and in 1884 he suffered a further blow when his wife, Nellie, died shortly after giving birth. Weakened by the strain of riding in the 1886 Cambridgeshire (in which he was beaten by a head carrying 1lb overweight) Archer contracted a severe chill and fever. Reduced both physically and mentally, in November 1886 Archer put a revolver in his mouth and, despite the desperate effort of his sister to stop him, pulled the trigger. An inquest found he had been 'temporarily insane'. He was just 29.

The sad story of Fred Archer has a strange link to the meeting at Galleywood in 1879 where he rode an easy winner. While walking across the course he was accosted by a gypsy woman who asked him to cross her palm with silver. What happened next was reported in the *Essex Newsman* a few days after his death:-

'He (Archer) laughingly did so, and the old crone, muttering to herself the while, glanced at his palm and immediately dropped it saying, "A sudden end, young gentleman, and by your own hand."'

Archer was said to have laughed loudly at the prophesy and went rejoicing on his way. His death caused massive public interest. The *Times* newspaper noted:- 'Frederick Archer might well have laid claim to the distinction of being one of the most famous men of the age.' The paper's correspondent said he didn't know of any other event in the sporting world that would have created so much interest 'among not only followers of the turf but the public generally as the tragic death of Archer... '

Along with Archer, two other jockeys dominated flat racing in the nineteenth century – Nat Flatman and George Fordham. They, too, rode winners at Galleywood and coincidentally both also died early. The three between them took forty jockey's championships and achieved the kind of celebrity status reserved for footballers and TV personalities today.

George Fordham

Flatman, who was born in Suffolk in 1810, became the first British Champion Jockey. His career lasted more than 30 years and by the 1840s he was the country's leading rider taking the championship for thirteen years in a row. Among a string of victories at home and abroad he won the Derby in 1844 as well as winning the St Leger and the 1,000 and 2,000 guineas three times each. By the 1850s Flatman was past his prime but he kept riding until in 1859 a post-race accident brought about his death at the age of 50. Accounts vary but on the way back to the weighing room he either fell from his horse or was kicked after dismounting. As a result a rib was driven into his lung and infection followed. After a lingering illness he died in August 1860.

George Fordham was born in Cambridgeshire in 1837. He won the Derby in 1879, the Oaks and the Ascot Gold Cup five times each and the Grand Prix de Paris three times. He was Champion Jockey every year between 1855 and 1863 as well as winning the title in four other years in his own right and jointly once. One newspaper correspondent noted that he was not an elegant rider '…his seat being awkward and he had a curious way of carrying his shoulders very high. He appeared careless and slovenly, too, on his way to the post. His success was largely obtained, like that of the late Fred Archer, through being so generally entrusted with the handling of good horses which he undoubtedly owed to his unswerving honesty.' Fordham died in 1887 at the age of 50 after a long and painful battle with consumption. His death prompted the medical journal 'The Lancet' to the opinion that his fatal illness had been caused by 'the hard life incidental to the life of a jockey…… Exposure to chills, profuse sweatings and enforced starvation to get down to weight…'

In 1881 Chelmsford Races were in a financial crisis and to make matters worse the race for Queen Charlotte's Royal Plate was discontinued marking the end of royal patronage. This race had already been reduced from an annual to a biennial event when it was split with the meeting at Ipswich. (In fact, Chelmsford was more successful than many courses in keeping a royal plate for as long as it did. Their number had been decreased in 1875 although the value of those remaining was increased so for a time Chelmsford benefitted). The royal plates were finally abolished in 1887; having originally been introduced as a way of encouraging improvements in the breeding and supply of cavalry horses, they were by then thought no longer relevant. Towards the end of the century the Race Stand Company decided to convert the course to steeplechasing under

National Hunt rules but despite this racing continued to dwindle in the years before the First World War. During the war itself the grandstand was taken over for army billets and the common used as a training area. Twenty-five pounder guns were dug in opposite the grandstand as defence against Zeppelins. Some damage was clearly done by the military during the war and in 1917 they offered to pay the Race Committee £69.10s.9d to cover repairs to the grandstand. The committee was unimpressed and asked their secretary to see if he could get a better offer. Two years later the military offered a further £230 for other damage and this time it was accepted without argument.

In 1922 the Chelmsford Race Stand Company put itself up for auction and the sale particulars for the grandstand and associated property described the course as 'occupying the most charming position in the county with a splendid elevation, magnificent views for many miles and surroundings of great natural beauty.'

The course was bought by the Chelmsford Racecourse Company which immediately invested £10,000 (nearly half-a-million pounds today) on improvements. The old grandstand was renovated to provide accommodation for 1,200 people. A new grandstand was built which could accommodate another 700 and the course was widened. The revival of racing was deemed important enough for the event to make the sports pages of the *Times* which reported:-

'Galleywood Common is one of the highest and most picturesque spots in the eastern counties and a gloriously fine day helped to make the day's racing pleasant as well as interesting... the spectators' interests have been well considered by the new management and notable among the improvements is the members new stand and enclosure.'

The Army occupied the racecourse during World War 1.

'Then and Now:- Crossing Margaretting Road at the Eagle pub c1930 (above) and (opposite) a modern photograph from the same spot.

Racing again became popular during this period with thousands of spectators and special trains being laid on from Liverpool Street station in London to Chelmsford. The special trains were such an important feature that the start of the first race at one meeting had to be held up because of delays on the railway. In 1931 the *Essex Chronicle* said the races were established as among the most attractive and interesting in the eastern counties with 'big fields and excellent sport'.

The meetings were attracting top class horses; among the winners at Galleywood was Golden Miller who became the most successful Cheltenham Gold Cup horse ever. He won the race in five consecutive years from 1932 to 1936 and in 1934 became the only horse to win the Gold Cup and the Grand National in the same year. When he died his connection with Essex was maintained and he was buried at Elsenham Stud in the west of the county.

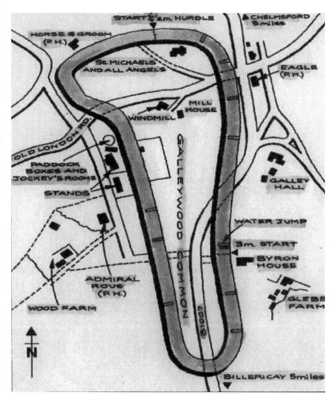

The racecourse layout in 1928.

However the resurgence failed to last and the crowds dwindled. The final meeting was held in March 1935, although the course was then converted to pony racing which survived until the beginning of the Second World War.

Golden Miller in 1934. Location unknown

Golden Miller, who raced at Galleywood, won the Cheltenham Gold Cup five times. He was laid to rest in Essex.

Chelmsford Races and the Upper Classes

Throughout the late eighteenth and the nineteenth centuries members of the aristocracy and the landowning classes played a key role in the promotion and running of horse racing across the country. They were influential at all levels in the sport – as promoters, administrators, owners and breeders. It was they who had the money, the time and the inclination to use racing as a way of enhancing their prestige. Contemporary newspaper reports underline the degree of their involvement:- aristocrats, titled officers (who often came from aristocratic backgrounds especially when commissions had to be bought) and 'esquires,' a term used fairly consistently to denote a wealthy land-owning background, dominate. Even those without titles had to be wealthy in order to participate since the total annual costs of keeping horses in training were high. Giving evidence to the Select Committee on Gaming in 1844, Richard Tattersall claimed that no one could keep a horse in training for less than £230 a year (around £22,000 today), not including jockeys' fees. Only about a third of horses running each season ever won a race and furthermore it has been estimated that generally about two-thirds of prize money came from the owners' pockets in the form of entry fees or forfeits for withdrawals. Even the most successful owners would be hard pressed to make a profit. For example, Lord Derby, who raced between 1842 and 1863, won a total of £94,003 in prize money but, since he had 243 horses in training during that period at an estimated average cost of £407 each, he actually spent £98,901.

At Chelmsford Races, prize money remained fairly constant throughout their history apart from a sharp rise during the heyday of racing in the middle of the nineteenth century. Taking representative meetings across the nineteenth and twentieth centuries total prize money was around £375 in 1803 (£30,000 today), in 1850 it was £445, (£42,000 today) it rose to £860 in the mid-1860s (£73,000 today) before falling to £240 in 1900 (£23,000 today) and rising slightly, although by less than inflation, to £350 in 1934 (£20,000 today), the year before racing ended. However in 1803 only 16 horses competed in the entire meeting whereas in 1866 four times that number took part so although the money on offer was considerably greater the odds of winning were greatly reduced. Even if an owner did win there were various ways of taking the prize money back. In the early years of racing winning owners were expected to contribute towards costs, defined as 'ropes, drums etc.'

As late as the middle of the nineteenth century a winner at Chelmsford was expected to contribute ten sovereigns (equivalent to around £950 today) back to the prize fund and put up another ten towards the prize money for the same race the next year. Even if an owner did manage to turn a profit at a day's racing in Chelmsford there was no guarantee he would keep it. *The Bath Chronicle* in August 1792 noted:- 'Mr Hammond, whose horse won the second day's plate at Chelmsford Races, returned home but little better for his expedition – for being stopped near Ilford by three footpads, he was stripped of a purse on the highway, equal almost in value to that which he gained on the turf.'

Heavy gambling was also a major element in the involvement of the upper classes in horse racing. There are no records of the amounts wagered at the meetings in Chelmsford but there are many examples of the scale of gambling on horses in the nineteenth century. Colonel Mellish, who won the St Leger in 1803 and 1804 and at one time had thirty-eight horses in training was said never to bet less than £500 (around £36,000 today) on a race and on many occasions even more.

George Payne, who was a leading figure on the turf for more than 40 years, inherited Sulby Abbey in Northamptonshire which brought him in as much as £17,000 a year in rents in addition to his £300,000 cash inheritance. He managed to lose £33,000 (£2,500,000 today) on the 1824 St Leger – remarking afterwards only that it was a pleasure to lose it. It appears that for the aristocracy and the landed gentry a major reason for participation in racing was not financial gain but as a form of conspicuous consumption and a way of underpinning their position in society. For the owners, the racehorse was the ultimate status symbol and a sign that they had money to spare with the racecourse rituals of the parade ring and winner's enclosure enabling horses and their owners to be displayed to the general public.

The upper classes could also use the races to underline their standing in other ways:- for example, men could be appointed a race steward, a prestigious honorary position awarded each year by the race committee. The stewards were responsible for the organisation of race meetings and for the implementation of rules and regulations, although before the professionalisation of racing their appointment was an acknowledgement of social position as much as racing expertise. They also played a key role in organising social events surrounding the race meetings and it was expected they would contribute wide-ranging financial support. In 1787 the Galleywood Race Stewards were the Right Honourable Lord Waldgrave and a Captain Harrison. Their account for expenses shows the degree to which they were involved in the social arrangements, with references to a ball and a public breakfast. They spent nearly £15 for 'a brace of bucks', more than £10 for 'fruit from London' and more than £20 for three night's music. Their total expenditure was more than £130 which equates to more than £14,000 in today's terms. It is not known whether or to what extent they were reimbursed by the race committee for this expenditure but there is evidence that on other occasions stewards did make substantial financial contributions. In 1814, for example, they subscribed ten guineas each (more than £800 today) and in 1836 they donated £50 (more than £4,000 today) in prize money for a race run in their name. As early as 1833 the Chairman of the Race Committee, Sir John Tyrell claimed that the financial burden involved in being a race steward 'frequently deterred gentlemen from accepting the office'.

In 1848 the costs involved in taking up the post of steward meant no one volunteered. The race committee decided to raise a subscription to bring in money to cover the necessary expenses. The *Chelmsford Chronicle* reported the committee's expectation that the appeal 'in support of this national amusement would be responded to.' The report noted the subscription had already had some success with a number of donations varying between two guineas and £10 (around £200 - £900 in today's terms) already received. In addition, one steward had already been found for the following year. He was John Watlington Perry of Moor Hall in Harlow who was clearly wealthy enough to bear the financial burden. He would later donate around three thousand pounds (worth a quarter of a million pounds today) towards the restoration of the parish church of St Mary and St Hugh in Harlow.   Another example of the involvement and financial contribution of the race stewards can be found in a *Chelmsford Chronicle* report in 1839:-

'The concert at the Shire Hall ... had excited great anticipation among all the admirers of that enchanting art, which "leadeth the senses captive to a sound", and the result fully realised the word of promise which the programme of the performances had given, rich as it was in gems from Italian and English composers, coupled with the names of many of our favourite vocalists. The stewards of the races had undertaken to cater for the public on the occasion and they discharged the duty in a manner which everyone felt had laid the assembly under a deep obligation to their liberality and taste; and with this successful example before them, their successors, we hope, will make a concert on the same scale an essential part of the proceedings of the Race week...The two parts of the concert were agreeably divided by a liberal supply of refreshments and the gratification afforded to nearly 300 participators of the feast of music is the most grateful acknowledgement that can be offered to the arrangers and promoters of the treat.'

Forty-five years earlier the stewards had been responsible for providing dramatic entertainment:- 'The moving plays at the theatre, under the patronage of the stewards, were very brilliantly attended and produced an assemblage of the elegant and beautiful in abundance'.
The attendance of the race stewards was seen to be a vital part of these social events and there had been some dismay at one meeting in 1865 when neither steward was able to attend a race ball – one by enforced attendance at the House of Lords and the other with 'an inflammation in his eyes'.

An indication of the status of those becoming stewards can be judged by the example of Cornelius Kortright who held the position in 1800 and had bought the nearby Hylands House estate in 1797. Hylands consisted of a large house surrounded by some 200 acres of land laid out as park and pleasure grounds with three farms occupying several hundred acres more.

The estate also carried with it the lordship of the manor of Shackstones. Kortright was of Danish origin and had owned several large estates in the West Indies and it is probable he had grown rich using slave labour to produce sugar on his plantations.

Hylands House has been restored to look as it did in the time of Cornelius Kortright

The scale of Kortright's wealth was such that between 1797 and 1803 he was able to employ Humphrey Repton, one of England's foremost landscape gardeners, to transform the entire estate. It is not surprising, therefore, that Kortright moved rapidly to assert his position in society by becoming a Chelmsford Race Steward and although his stewardship lasted only one year he continued to subscribe to the races with records as late as 1814 showing a donation of five guineas (more than £300 today).

He clearly maintained his social standing and in January 1810 the *Essex Herald* reported:- 'On Tuesday last Mr Kortright gave an elegant ball and supper at his beautiful seat, Highlands (sic) ... at which all the fashionables of the neighbourhood were present, including many military gentlemen.

About one hundred sat down to the supper tables, which were covered with every delicacy of the season, after which dancing was kept up till daylight appeared the next morning.'

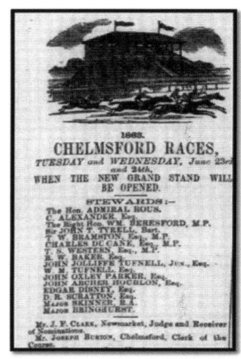

1863 Chelmsford Chronicle advertisement showing race stewards were still being drawn from the elite.

Another steward around this time was John Hanson, who lived at Great Bromley Hall, and officiated in 1796. He came from a successful family business in London and moved out to a large Essex country house, later becoming a Justice of the Peace, Deputy-Lieutenant of the county and commander of the local volunteer cavalry. As late as 1887 the race stewards were still firmly members of the upper classes, including, among others, the baronet and High Sheriff of Essex, Colonel Tufnell Tyrell and General Sir Evelyn Wood. Sir Evelyn was a distinguished soldier who was born at Cressing near Braintree in 1838. At the age of 20, while serving in India, he was awarded the Victoria Cross and eventually became a field marshal. In 1887 he was in charge of Eastern Command, based in Colchester and in 1903 he was given the freedom of the Borough of Chelmsford.

Sir Evelyn Wood VC

Wealthy individuals could also make an important contribution to the race meetings and so support their social position without having an official role in their organisation. In 1849 William Honeywood, who would later become Sheriff of Essex not only put up £25 in prize money for one of the races but also presided at one of the evening dinners. In 1873 his widow was still involved as a sponsor of one of the races and in providing venison for race committee dinners (for which the committee passed a vote of thanks). A broader indication of the social status of those subscribing to the races can be found by looking at some of the names on a list published in the *Chelmsford Chronicle* in 1814. Among them was R.A. Crickitt the senior partner in the Chelmsford bank, Crikitt's. His bank was caught up in the financial panic of 1825-26 when some 27 English Country Banks failed. An indication of his wealth can be found in a report of his bank's examination in bankruptcy. It was revealed that he had apparently used the bank to fund his political career and personal lifestyle and over an eighteen-year period had been paid £57,500 (more than £3,500,000 today) in profits from the family's banking interests in Colchester, Ipswich, Chelmsford and Maldon. He had represented Ipswich in Parliament from 1807 to 1811 and his electioneering expenses alone were estimated at £10,000. (More than £630,000 today). He also gives an indication of the tight knit nature of the upper echelons of Chelmsford society at that time – in 1813 he married Juliana Kortright, the daughter of Cornelius Kortright, the owner of Hylands estate mentioned above. Another subscriber on the list is Sir H.P. Mildmay, a member of the family who had bought the two manors of Chelmsford and Moulsham from the Crown in the fifteenth century. The subscription list also includes John Crabb, the town's resident magistrate. The races were an important occasion not just for the elite of Chelmsford; they drew support from the upper classes across the county. Among those attending in August 1836 was C.T. Tower who lived at Weald Hall in South Weald and was described in a nineteenth century history of Essex as 'lord of most of the parish' and owner of a mansion in 'one of the most beautiful spots in Essex' Also present were J.A. Houblon who owned Hallingbury Hall near Bishops

Stortford. The Houblon family were extremely wealthy having invested in the Bank of England at its foundation; one of them had been its first governor and two others were among its original directors. Also at this 1836 meeting was R.H. Abdy, of Albyns near Stapleford Abbotts, a house described as a 'fine stately mansion, standing in a pleasant park, said to have been built by Inigo Jones.'

There is also evidence that local politicians used the races to their own advantage. A study of race funding nationally, using the Racing Calendar for 1839, shows MPs were key contributors alongside the local aristocracy, gentry, local town subscribers, innkeepers, tradesmen and the government (in the form of royal plates). Local MPs were able to demonstrate their generosity and concern for a popular local event and to profit politically from their support for it. The national picture applied equally to the races at Chelmsford and there is clear evidence of the widespread involvement of local MPs in them. The meeting in August 1836 was attended by no fewer than six and a few years earlier a post-race dinner at the Shire Hall was attended by both the MP for the county and the member for Maldon. The financial contribution of MPs to the races is demonstrated by newspaper reports which indicate they added as much as £50 to prize money for individual races. This financial patronage by local MPs continued well into the nineteenth century and Race Committee minutes in 1878 noted a contribution of 'fifty pounds given by the Members of Parliament for the western division.' The following year a similar contribution was reported in the *Chelmsford Chronicle*.

John Bullock, the MP for Maldon

The view that the races were important to the political process in and around Chelmsford is supported by a controversy in 1833 when a meeting of prominent town citizens was called to discuss a request from the Race Committee for increased contributions. This turned into an attack on Sir John Tyrell MP who was chairman of the committee and was reported to have failed to pay his own subscription to the races since his election to Parliament. One speaker said that Sir John had become 'somewhat lukewarm' with regard to the interests of the town since his return for the Northern Division, however the speaker was unwilling to believe Sir John could 'so soon forget the debt of gratitude he owed to the inhabitants [of Chelmsford] for their support during the election of 1830, when he was first returned to represent the county. On that occasion, out of eighty-three persons in Chelmsford who voted sixty-nine gave the Hon. Baronet their suffrage'.

Race stewards were often drawn from among the ranks of local MPs and this tradition began early in the history of the meetings. In 1765, for example, it was announced that one of the stewards for the following year's meeting would be John Bullock, the MP for Maldon. (see previous page)

One of the most interesting of these politician stewards was Charles Du Cane of Braxted Park near Witham. Born in 1825 and educated at Charterhouse and Exeter College, Oxford, he later played first class cricket for the MCC as a batsman. In 1852 he was elected MP for Maldon but his election was declared void after it was found that his agents had been involved in bribery, although Du Cane himself was cleared. In 1857 he became MP for Northern Essex and held the seat until it was abolished in 1868. His name appears among the Galleywood Race Stewards in the late 1850s and early 1860s. He went on to become Governor of Tasmania which prospered during his tenure. After he returned to England he was knighted and died at Braxted Park in 1889 at the comparatively early age of 62.

Sir Charles Du Cane, race steward, MP for Maldon and later Governor of Tasmania

In addition to Du Cane, among those who stood for the two Maldon parliamentary seats at various times were members of the Bramston, Houblon, Strutt, Tufnell and Western families and these are all names that crop up regularly in connection with the races. Furthermore, those contesting seats across the county were also invariably drawn from landed families, many of whom also had strong links to the racing at Galleywood.

A Big Social Event

In the early years, the races were not only a sporting occasion but also an inspiration for a wide range of cultural and social events which were timed to coincide with them. There are indications at the beginning of the nineteenth century that the races themselves may have been of secondary importance to these social occasions. There were many reports of the low number of horses entered and sometimes a single entry in a race resulted in a walkover. In others the lack of any starters resulted in the race being cancelled. Consequently, one newspaper report in 1815 described two days of racing as 'very uninteresting' while the 'balls, public breakfasts and theatre were very fashionably attended'. It is clear from contemporary reports that it was important for the status of the town that these events attracted as many of the upper classes as possible. There is also an implication that the wealthy middle class*, who also attended these functions but lacked the social status of the aristocracy and gentry, would benefit from being present.

At this time these people were referred to as the 'middling sort'. They ranked well below the aristocracy and landed gentry and although they had money it was earned from activities such as trade and farming.

In 1816 the *Chelmsford Chronicle* noted:- 'The company each day was very numerous; the dinners and assemblies were well attended and the theatrical amusements attracted much attention. Upon the whole, we consider that our town has been honoured with a greater number of the nobility and gentry than upon any similar occasion for a number of years.'

The Duke of Wellington.
Master of the field at the Battle of
Waterloo

Four years later a reporter noted:- 'We were much gratified in observing so numerous an attendance at the Balls, Breakfasts and Dinners, the families of the nobility and gentry resident in the county in particular appeared to be assembled upon the present occasion more generally than at any period in our recollection.'

One ball was attended by a duke, a marquis, three lords as well as a number of MPs. In 1814 the Duke of Wellington was among the spectators at the races and news of his impending presence prompted the *Chelmsford Chronicle* to predict:- 'the most brilliant attendance that has been witnessed for a great number of years.' As early as 1767 The *Ipswich Journal* reported that the ball on Monday of the August meeting was the most brilliant it had known for years and its attraction for the top echelons of society is indicated by the fact that it was opened by Lord Petre and Lady Huntingtour.

The name of Lord Petre crops up repeatedly in connection with the races throughout their history as successive holders of the title were involved with them in one capacity or another. In the mid-1800s the then Lord Petre (William Henry Francis, the 11th baron) also founded and was

William Henry Francis, the 11th Baron Petre

patron of Writtle Races. For a time they flourished with attendance estimated by the *Chelmsford Chronicle* in 1846 at little short of 10,000 people. The paper noted that this was a far greater crowd than had been seen at Galleywood in recent years. However, with the death of Lord Petre in 1850 the races disappeared. The Petres were members of one of England's leading Roman Catholic families, their main residence was (and remains) Ingatestone Hall, around six miles from Chelmsford.

In 1794 the social events attracted a particularly large contingent from the aristocracy and again Lord Petre was among them. The *Chelmsford Chronicle* noted:- 'The balls were honoured with the presence of Lords Petre, Maynard, Hardwicke, Albemarle and their respective families; also by a very numerous train of the first beauty and fashion of the county ...'

The success of these social events is a recurrent theme throughout this period. In 1789 the *Chelmsford Chronicle* had reported:- 'At the public breakfasts and balls there were as numerous and brilliant a company as has lately been seen on the like occasion.'

Cultural events were also an important part of race meetings from early in their history. In 1767 The *Ipswich Journal* carried an advertisement for a concert to be held in the assembly room at the Black Boy Inn to coincide with the second day of the meeting. This was to consist of vocal and instrumental music including violin solos and a concerto for the harpsichord. 'The whole assisted by several eminent performers'. In 1772 the editor of the *Chelmsford Chronicle* welcomed news that the installation of a new organ in Chelmsford Parish Church was to coincide with the July race meeting and that two oratorios were to be performed. He predicted that the event would be the 'grandest of anything of the kind ever seen in this county' and noted that the nobility and gentry who usually frequented the races had long complained that 'some morning amusement was wanting.' Sadly the organ was not installed in time and the oratorios were cancelled.

However, the following year the town acquired a professional organist and when he learned how disappointed the Chelmsford race-goers had been by the cancellation he announced his intention to give a concert at the Black Boy Inn during the 1773 July meeting. This included a special song 'The Race' which he had composed himself. The reception he received for this concert encouraged him to arrange similar events every year from 1774 to 1777, always with leading musicians from London. Theatrical performances were also often timed to coincide with the races with some then continuing for a season of several weeks. From 1792 a large brick building in the town, originally built as an auction house, became a theatre. Other venues for plays were the assembly rooms of the larger inns which could hold two or three hundred people.

Chelmsford High Street around 1890. The building on the right was the site of the Black Boy – scene of many race balls and dinners.

In 1774 the Sadler's Wells Company appeared in Chelmsford during the race meeting and in 1779 'Mrs Baker's Company of Comedians' performed in the Chelmsford Theatre during July and August with shows every night on race days. More than fifty years later the *Chelmsford Chronicle* reported that on one race day the 'theatre was crowded to an overflow' although on this occasion the nature of the entertainment is not recorded. In addition to the balls and theatrical performances a number of 'ordinaries' were held to coincide with the races. These were meals provided at public houses at a fixed time and for a fixed price. The significance of these social events can be gauged by the fact that even small newspaper advertisements for the races, which gave details of how horses could be entered, also carried announcements for the associated attractions. These were clearly important events as early as the 1760s and also a way to attract women to the races. One advertisement, in 1761, announced:- 'On Monday night will be a ball and ordinaries for

the horses will not be permitted to run.
All disputes to be determined by the Stewards, or whom they shall appoint, and their decision to be final.
The Clerk of the Course will attend as usual at the Common, on the Friday and Saturday before the races, to let the ground for booths, stalls, &c.; and the ground must be paid for before they are erected.
The trainers or persons attending the horses are particularly requested to mention the colours of the riders at the time of entrance, for the purpose of inserting them in the list of the day.
All stakes must be made at Chelmsford.
       D. MAGENS, Esq. } *Stewards.*
       W. TUFNELL, Esq. }
Mr. S. BAKER, Veterinary Surgeon, Clerk of the Course.
Mr. CLARK, of Newmarket, Judge of the Races.
N.B. A PUBLIC DINNER at the Shire Hall, on TUESDAY; and on WEDNESDAY a PUBLIC DINNER at the Black Boy, for Ladies and Gentlemen : and a BALL at the Shire Hall in the Evening. BREAKFASTS on the WEDNESDAY and THURSDAY as usual.
Ladies' Tickets to the Ball 9s.—Gentlemen's 14s.—Breakfasts 3s.

This advertisement for the races is from the Essex Standard in July 1841 and illustrates the importance of the associated social events. It lists two dinners, a ball and two breakfasts the ladies, as usual, at the Black Boy and Red Lion.' The following night a musical concert and another ball were offered in the town.

So important were these ancillary events that newspaper reports of the races often began with accounts of them rather than the results of the racing itself. For example, an article on the meeting in August 1764 begins with news that at the ordinary at the Saracen's Head '... the company were entertained by a very large Turtle, presented by J. Luther esq., ... and at the ball the same evening the company was very numerous and brilliant, and the same the two succeeding nights.' The mention of a turtle here is in itself significant as at this time there was a well-developed market for them.

This had been in existence from as early as 1753 when *Gentlemen's Magazine* contained several accounts of large sea turtles being displayed in London public houses. Demand for turtles grew so significantly that they were transported alive from the West Indies on ships with specially constructed wooden tanks and an association between turtle soup and upper class pretensions developed fairly quickly.

By eating turtle those attending the dinner were associating themselves and by extension the races with the pinnacle of fashionable society and this gives a clue to the popularity of these events. They not only provided the aristocracy with a further opportunity to underline their position at the apex of society, they also allowed the middle classes beneath them an opportunity to mix with the elite and to gain an insight into their values, manners, codes of behaviour and tastes.

The Black Boy Inn in Chelmsford High Street. The scene of many concerts, balls and dinners held in conjunction with the races at Galleywood. It was demolished in 1857.

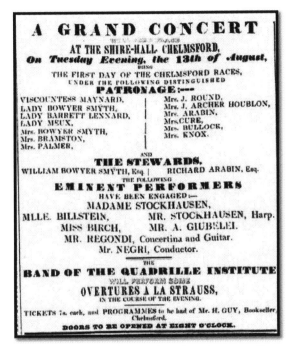

A GRAND CONCERT
AT THE SHIRE-HALL CHELMSFORD,
On Tuesday Evening, the 13th of August,
BEING
THE FIRST DAY OF THE CHELMSFORD RACES,
UNDER THE FOLLOWING DISTINGUISHED
PATRONAGE:—

VISCOUNTESS MAYNARD,
LADY BOWYER SMYTH,
LADY BARRETT LENNARD,
LADY MEUX,
Mrs. BOWYER SMYTH,
Mrs. BRAMSTON,
Mrs. PALMER,

Mrs. J. ROUND,
Mrs. J. ARCHER HOUBLON,
Mrs. ARABIN,
Mrs. CURE,
Mrs. BULLOCK,
Mrs. KNOX.

AND
THE STEWARDS.
WILLIAM BOWYER SMYTH, Esq. | RICHARD ARABIN, Esq.
THE FOLLOWING
EMINENT PERFORMERS
HAVE BEEN ENGAGED:—
MADAME STOCKHAUSEN,
MLLE. BILLSTEIN,   MR. STOCKHAUSEN, Harp.
MISS BIRCH,   MR. A. GIUBELEI.
MR. REGONDI, Concertina and Guitar.
Mr. NEGRI, Conductor.
THE
BAND OF THE QUADRILLE INSTITUTE
WILL PERFORM SOME
OVERTURES A LA STRAUSS,
IN THE COURSE OF THE EVENING.
TICKETS 7s. each, and PROGRAMMES to be had of Mr. H. GUY, Bookseller, Chelmsford.
DOORS TO BE OPENED AT EIGHT O'CLOCK.

This Chelmsford Chronicle advertisement for a concert to be held on the first day of the August race meeting in 1839 suggests it was very much an event for the wealthy

This was vital information for those who aspired to move up the social ladder and in modern terms the races and their associated social functions can be seen as an opportunity for 'networking'. The popularity of the social occasions associated with the races continued well into the nineteenth century and attracted the elite from across the county.

At the July meeting in 1837 a dinner at the Shire Hall was reported to have been attended by nearly 60 ladies and gentlemen and a ball the following evening by '150 fashionables'. In addition the stewards of the meeting attended a performance at the theatre. These occasions were very much the preserve of the wealthy middle and upper classes. An advertisement for a race ball to be held at the Shire Hall in 1839 puts the price of tickets for ladies at seven shillings and for men 13 shillings. In the same newspaper an advertisement for a grand concert on the first day of the races, also to be held at the Shire Hall, puts admission at 7 shillings and emphasises its 'distinguished patronage', which included four titled ladies and the stewards. A year earlier public dinners at the Shire Hall and Saracens Head were priced at nine shillings for ladies and 14 shillings for gentlemen. Public breakfasts were three shillings for men and women. At this time an average farm labourer's wage was less than two shillings a day.

However, by the middle of the century the social occasions were declining. In 1850 the *Chelmsford Chronicle* noted during the July meeting that the ball on the Wednesday was not as well attended as had been expected, especially as the ballroom was being used for the first time since its renovation.

Even so about 90 people - described as 'fashionables' did attend. The public dinners also attracted a smaller attendance than expected and the organiser, Sir John Tyrell, commented on 'the scanty support he had received, alike from the gentry of the county and from the town residents'. Although the importance of the races and their associated events dwindled over time they continued well past the middle of the nineteenth century.

A newspaper advertisement for the meeting in June 1863 includes an 'ordinary' at the White Hart and a Grand Race Ball. This was to be held at the Shire Hall under the patronage of the stewards and the 'ladies of the county.' In 1864 an evening of amateur theatricals held at the Chelmsford Corn Exchange in conjunction with the races was reported to have attracted 800 people with the 'stalls and the reserved seats being filled by a brilliant assemblage of the beauty and fashion of the county.'

Even at the end of the nineteenth century Galleywood Races had connections that reached to the very pinnacle of society. Around the turn of the century the Earl of Warwick was a steward at several meetings and his wife was one of the great socialites of her time. Frances 'Daisy' Maynard was born in 1861 at Easton Lodge near Great Dunmow. She married Francis Greville, Lord Brooke, who became the Earl of Warwick in 1893. She embarked on a number of affairs not least with the Prince of Wales, later Edward VII, whose mistress she was for nine years. She became the subject of endless society gossip and later when the affair ended she attempted to blackmail the royal family by publishing intimate letters written to her by the future king.

Right, Daisy Greville Countess of Warwick

Damping down the track in the early 1900s.

Racing and the Working Classes

With the balls, concerts and dinners beyond their reach, it was the race meetings themselves which were the major attraction for the working classes. In 1832 the Chelmsford Chronicle anticipated '...a numerous attendance ... of those classes who take a lively interest in the pleasure these races afford, and who, on any other occasion, rarely leave their laborious occupations'. Although contemporary newspaper accounts give no indication of the size of crowds Chelmsford race meetings attracted, other than vague terms such as 'vast' and 'huge', evidence from other areas suggests the number of spectators could run into tens of thousands. An estimate of the crowd at a small steeplechase held in Blackburn in 1840, for example, puts the attendance at upwards of 20,000.

At one point Chelmsford Races were so popular that the Bishop of London postponed a planned confirmation service in the nearby village of Great Baddow until after the meeting was finished. It should also be noted that while income restraints within families usually ensured that only men could attend gate money events, unenclosed race meetings like Chelmsford, where admission was free, meant they were also an attraction for families and crowds were always a mixture of men, women and children. A look at disposable income among Essex labourers at the turn of the nineteenth century gives some idea of the value free entertainment would have been to them.

Figures from the Essex Record Office show that between 1790 and 1810 prices approximately doubled but wages increased by a smaller proportion. Between 1785 and 1790 the average total weekly income of a labouring family was fourteen shillings (around £75 today), of this 48 per cent was spent on food alone. Between 1805 and 1815 the average total income had risen to twenty shillings but in real terms its value had decreased and the proportion spent on food had risen to 59 per cent.

Until the 1840s the races in Chelmsford were mainly local social gatherings. Unlike modern horse racing, gambling was of secondary importance since little information was available upon which to place a bet besides personal knowledge of horses and the appearance of the animal on the day. News travelled slowly, newspaper information was often out of date and, until the abolition of stamp duty on newspapers, expensive to obtain. So unless they had some racing connection, spectators could bet only on their instincts and very limited rationality and for that reason the carnival atmosphere of the meetings rather than the chance to bet on horses was the main attraction for the working classes.

In 1839 the *Chelmsford Chronicle* reported:- 'Independently of the racing the usual quantum of amusement was provided for children of all ages. Here Jim Crow won a grin from the gaping multitude and there a little man in a white hat, with a sharp nose and a sharper eye, won, through the instrumentality of thimble or ball, something more substantial from a rustic's pockets. Here the showman spread out his blandishments and spangles … while Ploughs, White Horses, Royal Oaks, Crowns and Anchors and Black Bulls innumerable invited the assembly to eat, drink and be merry'

The reference to the large number of booths selling alcohol suggests that drinking was an important part of the day's entertainment for many people. The idea that the meetings themselves were about more than just horse racing continued through the middle of the nineteenth century and beyond. In 1849 the *Chelmsford Chronicle* reported the entertainment going on well after the day's racing had ended with dancing booths 'gay with their lamps and illuminations'.

In 1858 the paper noted:- 'There was on the whole a large company upon the Common; a long line of country vehicles occupied one side of the course, a few dashing equipages were drawn up on the other – with the dark-eyed daughter of Egypt crossing the palms, and whispering random tales of moustached lovers into the ears of their fair occupants. The professor of "rouge-et-noir" penetrated the midst or hung upon the flanks of the crowd, for the special relief of those who found the weight of their cash inconvenient in the hot weather ...'

A decade later the carnival atmosphere still remained:- '... there were ... vendors of canes, correct cards and pencils; foolish gentlemen who sold purses with a lot of money in them for a shilling, and the equally foolish gentlemen who bought them; acrobats and tumblers, including one elderly gentleman, who we fancied we heard was about to lift half-hundred weights with his eyelids ... and another whose principal article of diet consisted of tow [coarse broken flax or hemp fibre], in which he indulged in great excess; gipsies to tell your misfortunes, Aunt Sally's, card-sharpers, roulette tables, betting men , including some who did pay and those who didn't and all the good and bad miscellany which complete the beauty and ugliness of the racing picture.

Boxing matches held during race meetings could be significant events in their own right. In 1820 a widely reported bout took place during the July meeting between Jack Scroggins and David Hudson. Little is known about Hudson but Scroggins, a London publican, was a successful bare-knuckle fighter in his day. He had taken part in matches for purses up to £100 (more than £7,000 today), running to 50 rounds and lasting two hours. (Bouts went on until one man was knocked out, retired, or his seconds threw in the towel.) However Scroggins seems to have been past his prime when he met Hudson at Galleywood for a purse of £25. Hudson was the victor in a bout lasting 11 rounds and a little over half an hour. Scroggins' loss was perhaps unsurprising given that one newspaper report described his method of training as one of 'debauchery' and he often drank brandy between rounds to revive himself.

Later descriptions of the racecourse suggest something akin to a fairground with fancy stalls and steam roundabouts. There are hints that the races were also an opportunity for more liberated behaviour than normal. A newspaper correspondent, reminiscing in 1868 about earlier days, wrote of '... The naughty people [who] made a saturnalia of it at night, and kicked about their heels until no end of the clock in the morning'.

In 1822 The Society for the Suppression of Vice reported its agents had brought to court five men for disseminating 'obscene hand bills' at Ealing, Winchester and Chelmsford race grounds and more than 900 had been seized and destroyed. The exact nature of these publications is unreported but the Society refers to another case involving 'copper-plate prints of the most disgusting obscenity' which retailed not only in this country but which were also exported to America.

Crime and Punishment

Horse races were a magnet for criminal behaviour of various kinds, the large crowds, with many people the worse for drink, made them an easy target. There are even suggestions that the presence of criminals at meetings across the country was part of their attraction for other race goers. The early twentieth century journalist and racing official, Jack Fairfax-Blakeborough, admired their technique, skill, self-confidence and amusing conversation while at the same time recognising the risk they posed.

At some meetings in Galleywood crime was rife; the July races of 1833 saw enough to fill an entire column in the *Chelmsford Chronicle* when the cases came to the Petty Sessions. The paper noted:- 'The number of swindlers, pickpockets, &c. who visited the course this year was very great, and their conduct during the first day became so daring that the high constable found it necessary to have more men upon the ground and issued orders to apprehend all the "thimble and pea men", and other suspected characters. No less than 20 persons including five women were in consequence taken into custody upon charges of picking pockets, vagrancy, &c. Today they were brought up for examination'. Although the women in this case were charged with vagrancy, the evidence clearly suggested they were involved in prostitution and contemporary accounts of other race meetings often refer to the presence of prostitutes. The mixture of drink, gambling and holidaymaking produced a ready clientele. In this case, having come from the racecourse, the women were found at a vagrant lodging house in the Moulsham area of the town 'in a most disgusting situation'. The constables told the court that the house was 'a perfect den of thieves and prostitutes – the door was left open all night in order that such abandoned characters might go in and out as they pleased and the house was in fact a complete nuisance to every person in the neighbourhood.' The women were convicted as vagrants and each sentenced to a month in prison. Whatever the charge, in most cases magistrates took a harsh view:- for example, one man accused of being involved in a theft at the July 1833 meeting described himself as a 'hay binder' and admitted that he had been in prison before for 'snaring' (poaching). One of the magistrates argued that a distinction should be made for those men, such as the accused, who were involved in the harvest and they should be sentenced to shorter periods so they did not lose the chance of employment. However, the rest of the Bench disagreed and the man was committed to prison for a month. The vast crowds offered many opportunities for pickpockets and organised groups travelled from meeting to meeting to ply their trade.

In 1831, the *Chelmsford Chronicle* reported:- 'Of pickpockets the number was unprecedentedly large'. The degree of crime at the races demanded a high police presence. Including, at one meeting, the Essex Deputy Chief Constable and a superintendent as well as a 'strong posse of police'. Not all crime was planned:- at a meeting in the early part of the nineteenth century an army captain, preparing to take part in a race, became the unfortunate victim of a bizarre opportunist crime. As a newspaper report put it:- '...in stripping in a hurry to mount he gave his coat to a man, supposing him to be his own servant, in which was his pocket book containing £400 in bank notes, with which the fellow immediately decamped.' That's the equivalent of having more than £30,000 stolen today. As noted earlier, betting on horses didn't become popular until 1840s but it soon became the centre of most crime at the races. As early as 1844 official action had been needed to control it.

View of the Old County Gaol in Chelmsford across the Stone Bridge. Early offenders at Chelmsford Races risked ending up here. The building was demolished in 1859 -- it was one of two prisons in Chelmsford which Charles Dickens thought were big enough to hold all the inhabitants of the county.

The *Chelmsford Chronicle* reported:- 'In obedience to the orders of the magistrates all gambling was thoroughly suppressed, which added greatly to the peace and good order on the ground; and if this rule be persisted in, as there is little doubt it will be, it will, by putting an end to a destructive system of what appeared to many legalised plunder, remove one great objection that has been urged against the races.' Clearly this crack-down on gambling failed to work and 'welchers' 'bookmakers who could not or would not pay – were a recognised feature of racecourse life. By 1879 the Jockey Club was employing a team of men, many former detectives, who travelled from race meeting to race meeting to identify them. Their job was to spot known welchers and eject them from grandstands and enclosures. In a court case involving one such individual, a solicitor noted:- 'if there is to be anything like respectability at race meetings it is absolutely necessary that welchers and such people should not be admitted to the grandstand.' Despite this, the problem remained and thirty years later, in 1910, 'welchers' were still appearing in court. One case involved a man who had set himself up as a bookie and took four shillings (about £18 today) from a customer at three to one. The horse won but when the punter returned the bookie had disappeared.

The problems with illegal gambling extended beyond welchers in the grandstand:- a notice to race goers circulated in 1884 warned that 'special constables have been appointed with authority to suppress and prevent all unlawful gambling and disorderly conduct.' The notice said that 'Thimble tables', 'E.O. Tables' and all other instruments of unlawful gaming will be taken away or destroyed and all persons offending will be prosecuted and punished by order of the magistrates' clerk. (Thimbles was a swindling game using three thimbles where the spectators bet on which one had a pea under it. It was usually worked by groups of three to seven who pretended to bet, encouraged punters and dealt with complaining losers. E.O. was a game of chance, similar to roulette, where a ball fell into slots labelled E and O respectively.) The effectiveness of the clamp-down on these games is questionable and in 1886 the three card trick (a game based on the same principle as 'thimbles') was still in evidence with one man sentenced to a month's hard labour for operating it. A year later another man was in court for performing the three card trick at the races. On this occasion the prosecutor caused amusement by telling the arresting officer:- 'We don't know anything about it here' and demanding he show the court how it was done. To loud laughter the policeman declined. The defendant was less amused when he was sentenced to a month in jail with hard labour.

At the same session another defendant was charged with operating a game called 'Pricking the Garter'. This game, also known as 'Fast and Loose' dates back hundreds of years and is mentioned by Shakespeare. A long loop of rope or chain is twisted into an hour-glass shape and the victim must choose which of the two holes in the pattern to place their finger. The rope is then pulled tight and if the finger is held fast the victim wins. Needless to say, whichever loop they choose they never do. On this occasion the arresting officer said he saw several boys lose shillings. The accused admitted he knew what he was doing was illegal and he was sorry for it. His apology achieved little and he was jailed for a month. Into the twentieth century, illegal gambling became less of a problem but the races continued to be a magnet for criminals. In 1907 a Dr Martin of Chelmsford was relieved of a gold watch and chain and several other people were said to have lost property in a similar manner.

Although reports of dishonest behaviour at race meetings always centred on the crowd, there is no doubt that dishonesty also affected the racing itself. While nearly all racing insiders tried to indicate it embodied honest, respectable and sportsmanlike values the reality was otherwise. For example, horses were run when they were unfit or deliberately pulled up in order to influence their odds in later, possibly more valuable, races.

There is no reason to doubt that this behaviour affected Chelmsford Races to any lesser degree than others but proof is hard to find. However, a *Chelmsford Chronicle* report in 1810 gives a rare public hint that things were not always above board:- 'The racing on the first day did not afford the gratification expected of the Queen's guineas, two horses being withdrawn after the first heat and the plate won with seeming ease by Donna Clara, but it did not appear the contest was maintained with requisite exertion'. Another rare reference to possible dishonesty in the way horses were run at Galleywood can be found in a *Chelmsford Chronicle* report of an 1868 meeting which refers to horses being put on a 'laudanum diet' in order to slow them down. Laudanum is a drug based on opium.

A Diminishing Role in a Changing World

As noted above, in the early days of Chelmsford Races the competition between horses was only part of their attraction. Apart from the many social functions another key element was the spectacle of cockfighting and newspaper advertisements for the races at the end of the eighteenth century always included a reference to it.

COCKING

During the Three Days RACING at CHELMSFORD, THERE will be a great MAIN of COCKS fought at the SARACEN'S HEAD between the Gentlemen of NOTTINGHAM and ESSEX for TEN GUINEAS a battle and a HUNDRED the main.

GOVDALL for Nottinghamshire FISHER for Essex

Chelmsford Chronicle advertisement for cockfighting during June races in 1791

Cockfighting was popular because unlike horse racing and many other forms of gambling it was difficult to 'fix'; the result being entirely down to the aggression of an individual bird. The fighting cocks often represented different areas and were owned by rival land-owners. Matches, or 'mains' as they were called, could run across entire race meetings.

In 1767, for example, 43 cock fights were held between Chelmsford and Hornchurch during the August meeting, the birds representing Chelmsford being supplied by Lord Waltham and Colonel Wynyard. In 1777 a main was fought between Middlesex and Essex and in 1791 a great match was advertised to be fought between the gentlemen of Essex and the gentlemen of Nottingham with substantial prizes of ten guineas a battle, worth more than £1,200 today.

A contemporary image of a 19th century cockfight. The spectators, people, gentle and simple act like madmen!

There are no contemporary descriptions of cockfighting at Chelmsford races but descriptions of what went on elsewhere do exist. A particularly detailed account was written by a German visitor to England, Zacharias Conrad von Uffenbach, in the early eighteenth century and gives a good idea not only of the cruelty involved but also of the enthusiasm of the spectators:-

'When it is time to start, the persons appointed to do so bring in the cocks hidden in two sacks, and then everyone begins to shout and wager before the birds are on view. The people, gentle and simple (they sit with no distinction of place) act like madmen, and go on raising the odds... Then the cocks are taken out of the sacks and fitted with silver spurs... As soon as the cocks appear, the shouting grows even louder and the betting is continued. When they are released, some attack, while others run away... [and some] are impelled by terror to jump down from the table among the people; they are then, however, driven back to the table with great yells ... and are thrust at each other until they get angry. Then it is amazing to see how they peck at each other, and especially how they hack with their spurs. Their combs bleed terribly and they often slit each other's crop and abdomen with their spurs. There is nothing more diverting than when one seems quite exhausted and there are great shouts of triumph and monstrous wagers; and then the cock that appeared to be quite done for suddenly recovers and masters the other.'

Cockfighting had been popular since at least the twelfth century but from the mid-eighteenth century onwards there was a change in attitude towards animal cruelty largely driven by the upper classes. In a letter to the Gentleman's Magazine in 1789 a correspondent stated that cruelty to animals 'hurts the feelings of speculative individuals, who cannot help shuddering at the misery they are frequently obliged to be witness to; but which, to shew the difference between cultivated and uncultivated minds, proves a fruitful source of high gratification to the illiterate and vulgar bulk of mankind.' In 1802 the Society for the Suppression of Vice was created consisting principally of the professional classes and the lesser gentry. Their activities were aimed almost exclusively at acts of cruelty committed by the lower classes. They drew a distinction between the sports of the upper and lower classes and never denounced fox hunting which in addition to the foxes being killed sometimes resulted in horses being ridden to death. This theme of cruelty to animals being a lower class problem was prominent in the early nineteenth century when it was not only assumed to be an indication of a low state of mind but also a cause of it.

The legal status of animals was first brought before parliament in 1800 when a series of bills for their protection was introduced. These bills put the primary emphasis on the degrading influence that cruelty towards animals had on man's character rather than the intrinsic moral status of animals. These were the first of a series of animal cruelty bills introduced into parliament over the early part of the nineteenth century and whatever their motives they culminated in the abolition of cockfighting in 1849. As early as the 1820s cockfighting was said to be 'nearly obsolete' in many parts of the country although the last report of cockfighting at Chelmsford Races was in 1833. The end of cockfighting was the first of a series of changes which were to narrow the attraction of race meetings like those at Galleywood where it had been a key element.

In the early years of racing, the poor transport system significantly restricted the catchment area for spectators and horses alike. Most people attended only their local meeting unless they could afford the high cost of post-horses or coaches.

With the coming of the railway to Chelmsford in 1842 the races began to draw spectators from a wide geographical area and over time this had the effect of diminishing their importance to the town as a local social occasion. A vitriolic article in the *Pall Mall Gazette*, reprinted in the *Chelmsford Chronicle*, summed up the changes wrought on local race meetings by improved transport links:-

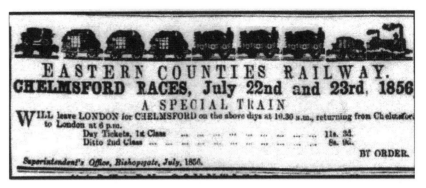

1856 Chelmsford Chronicle advertisement for excursion trains from London to the races

'The smaller country race meetings are gradually dying out, and it is quite well that they should do so... Before the introduction of the railways they formed pleasant occasions for a country holiday; they used to be attended by county families. Country gentlemen started their horses for the hunters' stakes and they often rode them themselves, and the meeting usually terminated with a county ball, at which everybody knew everybody else. But in these days of cheap locomotion the county element is utterly swamped by the blackguardism of the metropolis. The directors of Rattle and Smash Railway obligingly run cheap excursion trains from London for the occasion, laden with roughs and 'welchers', half the respectable people present are eased of their pocket books and watches before the day's sport is over, and the meeting now generally ends with a fight and a few burglaries which the local police are unable to prevent or detect'.

As far as the racing itself was concerned, in pre-railway days horses had to be walked between meetings and most raced only within a regional racing circuit. Meetings were held on week days as horses were walked between courses at weekends. However, fields often remained small with no more than a dozen horses running in a whole meeting and as late as 1825 at Chelmsford, with racing spread over three days, the August meeting attracted only 13 entries in all. The lack of entries was made up for by running races in heats, usually of three or four miles, and it was not unusual for a horse to run on two successive days. At the meeting in August 1825 one horse ran on all three days and managed to win on the third. Racing in heats bore little resemblance to modern horse racing. Because of the number of heats and the distances involved races often started at a trot, then moved into a canter and it was only over the last mile or so that the horses were kicked into a gallop. The number and frequency of the races each horse had to take part in tended to make them contests of stamina rather than speed and close finishes were a rarity.

In addition to increasing the catchment area for spectators, the coming of the railways brought major changes in racing itself. It meant horses could be transported quickly and easily by train which in turn led to a growth in the proportion of races for two-year-olds since previously these young horses had not been able to stand the strain of long-distance walking. Horses could travel to stables close to the races before meetings and thus decrease their chances of developing illness or injury or of being 'got at' on route. In the early 1800s most races at Chelmsford were run over two miles or more; the August meeting of 1804, for example, had no race shorter than two miles and one of four. As more young horses competed the length of races slowly reduced and by 1860 the only race of two miles was the Queen's Plate, all the others were of a mile or half-a-mile. The move towards shorter races also hastened the introduction of professional jockeys since younger horses running in shorter races were given light weights to carry and these were weights to which no portly gentleman of the period would think of reducing himself. The effect of these changes at Chelmsford is illustrated by the increase in entries for the main race, The Queen's Plate. Despite being worth a hundred guineas (more than £7,500 today), in 1799 and 1800 the race attracted only single entries and consequently the horses were awarded the prize by being required merely to canter round the course. The same thing happened a few years later causing some dismay among the crowd; one spectator noting 'it was truly vexing to observe the guineas so disposed of.' Less than forty years later the number of entries for the race was nearing double figures.

These changes also meant the races were no longer of purely local significance. The *Era*, a national newspaper noted for its sporting coverage, said of Chelmsford in 1852:- 'This little meeting, which has been gradually increasing in the estimation of the London sporting world, came off on Wednesday and Thursday in the presence of the most numerous and aristocratic attendance we have ever seen attracted to the beautiful domain of Old Galleywood.'

By the middle of the nineteenth century Chelmsford Races were still drawing large crowds but there was a feeling that change had not gone far enough and there were calls for improvements to the way the races were run and a clear demand for a more professional approach. There was also criticism of the lack of support from the wealthy local elite. In 1847 the Chelmsford Chronicle published an anonymous poem setting out the dissatisfaction:-

A Voice From Galleywood

Another year has passed away
Since last, my friends, we met;
Once more we've seen our August race
I fear with some regret.
The town was dull, the sport was slack,
The course was far from gay;
It seemed more like a funeral
Than Chelmsford's racing day.
I will not boast of scenery,
Such as stately Goodwood shews;
Or Ascot, whither royalty,
In all its splendour goes.
Yet I was fair and liberal,
Mine was no niggard's hand;
I freely offered all I had
To the sportsmen of the land.
I gave them what they most require,
Alike for man and horse,
A handsome sum with every stake –

And who will blame the course?
Then wherefore lacked I that support,
Which justly was my due;
I thought I had a host of friends,
But friends, alas, were few.
I look'd into that tott'ring stand,
The stewards' place was bare;
Bilton sold cyder and champagne,
But Perry[1] was not there.
And thou too, Maynard[2], noble born,
How have I injured you,
That thou didst shun my company,
And fled far from my view?
Why didst thou promise openly
To be my truest friend,
On whose support and patronage
I mainly might depend?

[1] *John Watlington Perry was a wealthy Essex benefactor – whether or not he was spurred into action by this criticism isn't known but two years later he agreed to become a race steward (see page 44).*
[2] *Viscount Maynard of Easton Lodge near Great Dunmow had strong associations with the races. His wife was patron of a number of race-day concerts. He was the grandfather of Daisy Maynard – later Countess of Warwick (see page 63).*

Just go to York or Doncaster
And there you'll surely see
How zealously the stewards act,
And what they ought to be.
The time for us to part my friends,
Unless some effort's made
To raise my dropping energies,
Ere I sink into the shade.
Then up ye men of Essex rise,
And merry maidens too;
If you will think of Galleywood,
I'll ever think of you.

A few years later, in 1853, a long article in the same newspaper noted:- 'The stand is to be rebuilt and better regulations have been introduced into the rules as to the ground. But amidst all this revival and reform it is felt that some changes should be made as to the regulations in the sports themselves.' The writer noted that Chelmsford had many advantages, being close to Newmarket, with a course that is 'as good and far better than many whereon the largest prizes are contested – its central situation amongst the stables of the south -- the increasing patronage given by the sporting community of England's better arenas – and the increasing disposition to extend that patronage, give to this meeting all the elements and constituents of success.' The writer described the management of the races as 'like the seedling thistledown, left to chance to rear its head when and how it will.' He complained that 'the present rationale of racing detail is little understood by those who manage in the locality and year after year the old style of things is consummated. It is really only requisite to look around and see what has been done and is doing at other meetings, adopt the same means and the usual attendants of success must follow.'

Within a decade the writer got his wish and in the 1860s Chelmsford appointed Admiral Henry Rous, the senior steward of the Jockey Club, to preside over the races at Galleywood. The changes he inspired led to this period being seen as the golden age in their history with newspaper reports in the mid-1860s speaking of a 'new era'. Rous, like most of elite of the racing world, had been born into the aristocracy. His father was Lord Rous, later the 1st Earl of Stradbroke who had a stud in Suffolk. After leaving the navy Henry Rous became an expert in handicapping and the rules of racing and in 1855 became honorary public handicapper. Surprisingly the rules of the day allowed him to bet on horses he had himself handicapped although his integrity was never called into question. By the early 1860s Rous had emerged nationally as 'dictator of the turf', he was seen as both high minded and practical and he did much to professionalise the sport and strengthen the power of the Jockey Club.

Admiral Henry Rous

One of his key reforms was to extend the powers of the stewards as he was particularly concerned with the way in which races were started. He had written as early as 1851:- 'Nothing can be more disorderly than the system at the provincial meetings. The starters are respectable men but notoriously incapable. They have no control over the jockeys, and the public is led to think the starter has a particular interest in a particular horse. Country Stewards will not support the starter by fining and suspending jockeys. Then there is a scene of disorder.' These scenes of chaos extended to even the major meetings and Rous commented that if the horses for the Derby succeeded in getting off within an hour it was 'considered a fair amount of business.' After a long campaign his views were finally accepted and in 1863 the powers of the stewards were extended so that they could not only fine those jockeys who took unfair advantage at the start but they could also suspend them.

Suspensions could only be lifted by the Jockey Club. The effect of this change was instantaneous with one observer noting:- 'It is almost difficult to believe that the obedient jockeys who last week assembled at the post, respectfully and with regularity, awaiting the orders of the starter, are the daring and lawless set who but a few weeks ago ... deliberately and impudently refused to acknowledge the official supremacy. The remedy for disobedience at the start has been discovered.' So influential was Rous that a book he wrote on horse racing was translated into French and the Sporting Life complained that the price of the English version was keeping it out of the hands of thousands of people who would otherwise be only too glad to refer to its authority. Apart from these general changes, there were others specific to Chelmsford and in 1864 *The Sporting Life* reported several major alterations to the course, including a fenced saddling enclosure which charged an entrance fee and changes which allowed horses to be dismounted near the weighing-in room without interference from the crowd. Clearly these improvements were viewed as significant in the racing world with the *Chelmsford Chronicle* reporting:- 'Members of the turf are warm in their praise of the arrangements and declare that the weighing-room, the paddock and the ring are more contiguous and convenient than on any other course in England.' Admiral Rous was also the force behind other changes to the nature of the races and the *Chelmsford Chronicle* noted after one meeting that the 'purely business part of the meeting reflects the highest credit on the officers, not a single hitch having occurred in any department.' The *Morning Post* commented:- 'throughout a due regard has been paid to punctuality ...The meeting has been successful in every point, and the managing committee have every reason to congratulate themselves...'

However, it was the professionalism that Rous brought to the races which may have been responsible for a change in their character which further narrowed their appeal and undermined their popularity with the sections of society to whom they had represented a major social event. In 1868 the *Chelmsford Chronicle* lamented:-

'If anything were wanting in evidence of the great contrast in the character and spirit of these as compared to the old days, the fact of Chelmsford having three meetings in the year forms conclusive testimony on the point. The quality of the sport is of course immeasurably improved ... Still the veteran supporters of the local turf may be excused for entertaining an affectionate veneration for former days when the old stand was a representative piece of sporting architecture, for there was once a time when the turf and gorse of Galleywood Common was trodden by more feet than now wend their way to be present on the spot – when Chelmsford Races were gala days for the people within twenty miles around, when the rails were fringed as far as the eye could reach with the carriages of the neighbouring gentry; and when "two to one bar one" was not the "be all and end all" of the meeting.'

As this suggests, despite the high professional regard in which the races were held during this period, there is evidence that the change in their character undermined their general popularity resulting in a failure to make a profit. The losses during 1868 were £424.10s (£34,000 today) and a special meeting of the Race Committee was called to discuss them. This deficit continued to grow; in 1869 the Race Committee's bankers granted a £300 overdraft (nearly £25,000 today) and in 1870 the company which owned the grandstand stepped in and handed over more than £100 (£8,500 today) to the committee to help cover their debts. There is evidence that among the methods used to raise money was a house to house collection of subscriptions and it is likely, as for other meetings around the country, contributions were sought from hoteliers, publicans, brewers and other local traders who stood to gain financially. However, by the 1870s the numbers attending were down and the number of meetings themselves reduced from two to one a year. And so the races were under attack on two fronts; they no longer represented the gala days they once did and despite their improved professionalism they were financially unprofitable. This second factor became increasingly important since, as contemporary observers noted, 'horse racing was becoming, every day, more of a business than a sport'.

The professionalisation of racing also brought increased costs in the form of wages for starters and other officials and these were in addition to the existing maintenance costs which had always been borne such as painting and decorating the stands, repairs to the rails and alterations to and maintenance of the course. Despite the increasing costs some opportunities to maximise income were missed. Nationally there were few meetings on Saturdays and none at all on Sundays and Chelmsford Races were usually run midweek. As Chelmsford became more and more industrialised, patterns of work and leisure changed and the increasing number of people working in factories with free time only at weekends inevitably decreased the potential number of spectators for mid-week race meetings.

Furthermore, as noted above, many spectators travelled to the races by train from London and this made them vulnerable to competition from other courses around the capital. That competition increased in the latter part of the nineteenth century with the introduction of enclosed courses which required an entrance fee from all spectators not merely those using the grandstands. The first was at Sandown Park in 1875 which was immediately successful. It began with two annual meetings but within two years had increased to four and by 1880 to five. Shortly afterwards Kempton Park opened followed in the 1890s by enclosed events at Hurst Park, Lingfield and Gatwick and in the early part of the twentieth century at Newbury. These new courses offered better facilities; almost all had a railway station within easy walking distance, often with a covered walk-way from the platform to the stands. Much of the racing was of a high standard, featuring top quality horses and jockeys and the tracks were kept in first rate condition so owners had no need to fear injury to their valuable horses.

Crucially these enclosed meetings were able to offer an increased level of prize money which in turn attracted more as well as better horses. Large fields were also attractive to spectators – as one contemporary racing writer commented:- 'Good management and good money mean good sport.' In 1886 Sandown introduced the Eclipse Stakes with a massive prize of £10,000 (nearly one million pounds today); this can be contrasted with prize money at Chelmsford where the total fund for an entire meeting never exceeded £1,000. Even small meetings were able to survive if they were able to charge general admission. Cartmel in the Lake District, for example, although coming into existence a century later, had a similar history to Chelmsford, converting to National Hunt racing at the end of the nineteenth century. However, it was on private land owned by the Duke of Devonshire and was able to start charging admission. In 1884 it was recorded that 7,000 people had paid to see a day's racing and the track has continued to flourish to the present day.

The Aristocracy in Decline

Another factor behind the decline of the races was diminishing support from the aristocracy and the county elite. Despite the disappearance of the many social events surrounding the races around the middle of the nineteenth century, continued upper class involvement in the races themselves was seen as crucial by contemporary commentators. In 1863, for example, the vice chairman of the Race Committee commented with satisfaction on reports that the new grandstand had been well patronised by the aristocracy of the county and he hoped this would continue. However, this was not to be the case and little over a decade later, in 1876, the *Chelmsford Chronicle* noted:- 'Only a few of the really representative people of the county figured in the grandstand'. This lack of upper class support was clearly of concern to those organising the races and in 1879 the Race Committee distributed a circular to those described as 'the county gentry.' In it the committee members were said to be:- '...very desirous that one of the oldest race meetings in the kingdom should not be allowed to die out without a strenuous effort being made to prevent it. They cannot but believe that this feeling will be shared by the county generally. It is, however, manifestly impossible for any committee to accomplish this desirable effect without the valuable assistance of the noblemen, gentlemen and other inhabitants of the county.'

This appeal did have a degree of success with subscriptions received from several members of the aristocracy as well as a number of landowners. However, this appears to be the last occasion the county elite rallied round to support the races and a similar appeal three years, in 1882, later produced only £150 (£13,500 today) with just one member of the aristocracy among those subscribing. He contributed £25 (£2,200 today) but some members of the landed gentry were not so generous:- Thomas Mashiter, for example, who owned a large estate at Hornchurch sent just five guineas (less than £500 today).

The decline in upper class support affected owners as well as spectators. Numbers are difficult to quantify but some general evidence can be drawn from the lists of owners published in the Racing Calendar. This suggests the proportion of upper class owners was constantly falling throughout the nineteenth century from 20 per cent in 1809 to 10 per cent in 1869.

At the end of the century other factors further eroded their importance to the sport. The aristocracy which led England until 1914 was a small but immensely powerful group; from 1869 until 1914 the number of aristocrats holding cabinet seats was never less than six and in the late nineteenth century rose as high as ten. A critical element to their power and status was the ownership of property in general and land in particular and as late as 1894 the editor of *Burke's Landed Gentry* was able to assert that land ownership was the principal 'test of rank and position'. However, from the 1880s the landowning class which did so much to support racing suffered a sustained and successful political assault. This was further accentuated by its economic decline and loss of property which in turn weakened its local position as the elite which had for centuries ruled the counties of England by hereditary right and unchallenged tradition. The extension of the vote led to a widespread rejection of old-fashioned rural politics while the creation of the new county councils brought a real change in the nature of local government. At the same time increasing financial worries meant many landowners were less inclined to shoulder traditional responsibilities or assume new ones.

The agricultural depression of the last quarter of the nineteenth century led to estates being broken up and sold and this break-up accelerated after the First World War accentuating the withdrawal of the upper classes from local leadership. Furthermore, Essex was not as endowed with landowners who might be able to withstand the changes as many other counties. In 1873 only eleven families in the whole of the county owned more than 3,000 acres.

The aristocrats and landed gentry were replaced to some degree by newly rich businessmen who set themselves up as country gentlemen on the traditional model and often became keen supporters of horse racing. Some established large racing stables and stud farms.

In 1924 just two members of the aristocracy were listed among the officials in the race programme

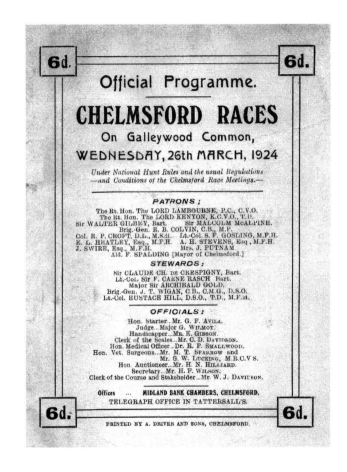

6d.   6d.

Official Programme.

CHELMSFORD RACES

On Galleywood Common,
WEDNESDAY, 26th MARCH, 1924

*Under National Hunt Rules and the usual Regulations
—and Conditions of the Chelmsford Race Meetings.—*

PATRONS :

The Rt. Hon. The LORD LAMBOURNE, P.C., C.V.O.
The Rt. Hon. The LORD KENYON, K.C.V.O., T.D.
Sir WALTER GILBEY, Bart.   Sir MALCOLM McALPINE.
Brig.-Gen. R. B. COLVIN, C.B., M.P.
Col. R. P. CROFT, D.L., M.S.H.   Lt.-Col. S. F. GOSLING, M.F.H.
E. L. HEATLEY, Esq., M.F.H.   A. H. STEVENS, Esq , M.F.H.
J. SWIRE, Esq., M.F.H.   Mrs. J. PUTNAM.
Ald. F. SPALDING [Mayor of Chelmsford.]

STEWARDS :

Sir CLAUDE CH. DE CRESPIGNY, Bart.
Lt.-Col. Sir F. CARNE RASCH, Bart.
Major Sir ARCHIBALD GOLD,
Brig.-Gen. J. T. WIGAN, C.B., C.M.G., D.S.O.
Lt.-Col. EUSTACE HILL, D.S.O., T.D., M.F.H.

OFFICIALS :

Hon. Starter...Mr. G. F. AVILA.
Judge...Major G. WILMOT.
Handicapper...Mr. K. GIBSON.
Clerk of the Scales...Mr. C. D. DAVIDSON.
Hon. Medical Officer...Dr. R. P. SMALLWOOD.
Hon. Vet. Surgeons...Mr. M. T. SPARROW and
Mr. G. W. LUCKING, M.R.C.V.S.
Hon. Auctioneer...Mr. H. N. HILLIARD.
Secretary...Mr. H. F. WILSON.
Clerk of the Course and Stakeholder...Mr. W. J. DAVIDSON.

Offices   **MIDLAND BANK CHAMBERS, CHELMSFORD,**
TELEGRAPH OFFICE IN TATTERSALL'S.

6d.   6d.

PRINTED BY A. DRIVER AND SONS, CHELMSFORD.

However, they knew much less about the world of horse racing and breeding than the traditional racing establishment and as a result trainers and stud farm managers, who had formerly been little more than paid servants, rapidly gained in status and power. Trainers rather than owners became responsible for determining when a horse ran and increasingly for the purchase of bloodstock. This all added to the increasing professionalism of the sport and by the end of the nineteenth century racing was changing from contests between horses owned and bred by knowledgeable, often aristocratic, men into an entertainment industry funded to a large extent by 'new' money. The changes were clearly visible in the Chelmsford meetings and from the late nineteenth century onwards aristocratic owners were notable for their absence. Although they continued to feature among the stewards, by the early part of the twentieth century their participation was dwindling there also. The meeting in March 1907, for example saw not a single aristocratic steward or other race official. They did make a brief return in the early 1920s – in 1923, Lord Lambourne and Lord Kenyon were listed among the race patrons and the Earl of Londesborough among the stewards, but again they failed to feature among the owners. Two owners who ran horses in the last meeting at Galleywood in 1935 demonstrate this move to 'new money'.

'New Money'
Arthur Sainsbury of the grocery store family

One of them was Arthur Sainsbury of the grocery store family. Sainsbury was one of 12 children of the founders of the company, John James Sainsbury and his wife Mary Ann. He became the firm's provisions buyer and managed the kitchens, becoming a director in 1922.

Another owner at the last Galleywood meeting was Bertram Mills, the circus entrepreneur. Mills was born in London in 1873, the son of an undertaker who was described as a 'pioneer of embalming'. He left school at 15 and joined the family firm before serving in the First World War. Afterwards he became interested in the circus and as the result of a bet formed his own circus company which quickly became a household name. Bertram Mills died in 1938 but his sons continued to run the circus which survived until 1967.

In 1932 Harry Gordon Selfridge, the proprietor of Selfridges department store in London, featured among the owners. Selfridge was a maverick American retailer who opened his eponymous Oxford Street shop in 1909 and found massive commercial success. He enjoyed a lavish lifestyle and was said to have a penchant for 'large

Bertram Mills:- His circus became a household name.

houses, fast women and regrettably slow horses.' His greatest addiction other than work was gambling which in one form or another dominated his life – whether it be risking all his money to build a store that was arguably at the wrong end of Oxford Street to the fortune he gambled on horses and in casinos. It is estimated that in the three decades he lived in London he squandered nearly £65 million pounds in today's terms on high living. Finally, in 1939, at the age of 83 he was ousted from the store. He died in poverty in a small flat in Putney.

Harry Gordon Selfridge:- A penchant for slow horses and fast women.

Another factor in the decline of aristocratic support for the races may have been the move at the end of the nineteenth century to National Hunt racing over jumps rather than flat racing. It is not clear from the race committee records why Chelmsford Races made the change, but it was probably connected to a decision by the Jockey Club to introduce a rule requiring minimum prize money of £300 a day for flat meetings (more than £26,000 today). This helped to eliminate many minor meetings and is known to have pushed some courses into National Hunt racing where the prize money regulations were less exacting. It seems probable that Chelmsford Races were among the meetings forced into a change since, as noted above, prize money was generally low throughout their history and the Race Committee minutes around this time make it clear they were in financial difficulties. Furthermore, it is known that the £300 prize money rule prevented any meeting taking place at Chelmsford in 1880.

The first reference to National Hunt racing at Galleywood appears in the race committee minutes in 1881; by 1883 the committee had decided to build a water jump and six years later took the decision to convert the course wholly to steeplechasing. National Hunt racing did not attract the social prestige of flat racing, having a reputation for being rough and dishonest. Control of racing at Galleywood to a large extent reflected National Hunt's tougher reputation with many of those running it having military backgrounds rather than being drawn from the aristocracy or the landed gentry. The Race Committee records from 1909 to 1922 show that a total of 30 members served during this period and of those ten held military rank. This is in contrast to the membership of the committee between 1867 and 1909 when a total of 37 men served, only two of whom had military rank. This increased control by military men extended to those officiating on the racecourse itself. A list of eleven senior race officials in 1932 included four of military rank, one of whom was a brigadier-general. A key figure in Chelmsford Races in the late nineteenth and early twentieth centuries was Sir Claude Champion de Crespigny and he demonstrates just how far removed those involved in steeplechasing were from the more genteel world of flat racing. Sir Claude, who lived at Great Totham, near Maldon, was a rider, steward, judge and member of the race committee. He was an extraordinary Victorian adventurer, described by the *Times* on his death in 1935 at the age of 88 as a 'Man of Honour and Sportsman'. He had served in the navy and then the army where he developed a life-long passion for steeplechasing, riding his last race at the age of 67. In 1883 he crossed the North Sea by balloon from Maldon and three years earlier had become the first European to swim across the great cataract rapids of the Nile, braving crocodiles to do so. He was also a fearless great game hunter and wrote to the *Essex Newsman* from Nairobi in 1905 saying that two man-eating lions were creating panic in a district 200 miles away and he and his son were 'just off to see if we cannot add their jackets to our collection'. At one point Sir Claude had been declared bankrupt.

Sir Claude de Crespigny:- Rode his last race aged 67

In 1904 he caused a furore when he wrote to the *Essex Chronicle* attacking his fellow race stewards as men who 'might make most worthy churchwardens or dancing masters at a girls' school, but [who] have something to learn as stewards of a steeplechase meeting'. Clearly, the character of Sir Claude was a far cry from that of the elite who had run racing at Chelmsford for much of the nineteenth century.

Gambling Puts on the Pressure

As horse racing became more professional and the social events surrounding it diminished, gambling became its central attraction. In the early nineteenth century excessive betting was illegal but in 1845 the Gaming Act removed betting from the criminal law. However, this led to a profusion of betting shops where wagers could be struck for cash and as a result in 1853 Parliament legislated again to outlaw public betting and restrict bookmakers. This in itself effectively discriminated against the poor who were unable to bet on credit or in clubs and as a result off-course betting was driven into the street where bookmakers laid bets through runners, who were often young children, and took money in pubs, workplaces and on street corners.

Local byelaws to some extent controlled street betting but the extension of press coverage of racing brought news and results to a wider public and also a host of advertisements for tipping services and credit betting by post. This sparked establishment fears of the damage being done by gambling to the working population and a belief that ordinary people could not be trusted to exercise judgement and discretion. As a result another Act of Parliament in 1906 prohibited the advertising of tips and postal credit betting. This meant that off-course betting was legally next to impossible for those of moderate means but straightforward for those able to afford a credit account. This led to an increase in the number of on-course bookmakers since the only way most people could bet was by physically going to a race meeting.

In 1928 the state owned Tote was set up to provide an alternative to the bookmakers, paying out better odds. The result of these changes, as Lord Ilchester was to note in the report of his committee set up in the 1940s to look at the future of horse racing, was to turn spectators into 'punters rather than race-goers'. This left racing vulnerable to pressure from other forms of gambling, notably greyhound racing and the football pools, both of which became massively popular in the 1930s.

The 1930s saw a boom in greyhound racing with many tracks at football grounds as was the case in Chelmsford. This advertisement is from the Chelmsford Chronicle in April 1933.

In the case of greyhound racing the decisive step came with the introduction of the electric hare at Belle Vue in Manchester in 1929. This attracted a crowd of 27,000 to the first meeting at which it was used and was quickly adopted at other tracks. It was a sport which lent itself to rapid expansion; the competitors could be bred and trained quickly and the capital investment to set up meetings was relatively modest. By 1930 there were sixty companies mounting greyhound racing across the country. Many football grounds had tracks around the outside of the pitch as was the case in Chelmsford. Greyhound races were particularly attractive to people whose betting tended to be small scale and they were far more frequent than horse race meetings. In the 1930s there was a boom in greyhound racing at stadiums in and around Chelmsford; in addition to the town's own track at Chelmsford Football Club there were meetings at Little Waltham, Maldon, Brentwood, Stondon, Southend and Romford. These were clearly successful and the local press, which carried the race results, reported large crowds. Similarly, the growth in football pools was outstanding and in 1934/35 as much as £20 million (well over £1bn today) was being staked annually.

Within two years this had doubled thanks largely to a high court ruling that a degree of skill was required to forecast results rather than chance which meant they avoided the provisions of the Gaming Acts. These outlawed off course cash betting on horse and greyhound racing. This in turn meant, crucially, that the football pools were the only form of gambling that could be carried out at home by post. No figures exist for the actual numbers 'doing the pools' in the 1930s but a government social survey in 1950 suggested 51 per cent of the male population and 28 per cent of women were participating. Neither was this a purely class based phenomenon with later research indicating significant participation across the social classes from around 44 per cent of upper middle class men to 60 per cent of upper working class men. It is impossible to prove a link between the boom in the alternative gambling opportunities afforded by greyhound racing and the football pools in the 1930s and the end of Chelmsford Races but it seems more than likely it was an important factor.

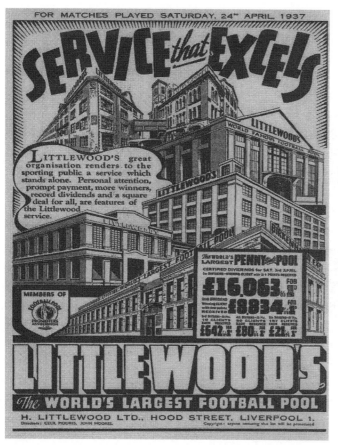

The increasing popularity of football pools was a likely factor in the demise of the races at Galleywood. This advertisement from 1937 was a regular feature in national newspapers.

Littlewoods claimed to be the 'World's Largest Football Pool'. At its peak the company employed over 10,000 people in Liverpool when unemployment nationally was over three million.

A Late Victorian Sporting Revolution

From the 1860s to the end of the nineteenth century there was a great boom in sport. This was mainly, although not entirely, a middle class phenomenon with a large transformation in the scale and nature of the country's sporting culture. The numbers of sporting clubs, governing bodies and other institutions grew rapidly and football, rugby, tennis and golf were all major leisure innovations.

In Chelmsford, The West Essex Bicycle Club was formed in 1875 and had its headquarters at the Saracen's Head. Three years later the Chelmsford Lawn Tennis and Croquet Club was founded as was the Chelmsford Football Club and the following year the Chelmsford Cricket Club was reformed (having previously existed as early as 1755). In 1893 Lord Rayleigh became the first president of the newly formed Chelmsford Golf Club –

The West Essex Bicycle Club was formed in 1875 and had its headquarters at the Saracen's Head in Chelmsford.

perhaps an indication that the aristocracy were beginning to broaden their horizons—and Chelmsford Hockey Club began in 1898. It is ironic that one of these new sports, golf, had a direct impact on the racecourse at Galleywood. In 1850 there were only 17 golf clubs in the United Kingdom, by 1898 there were 1,460, half of them in England – one of them at Galleywood. In 1893 the Chelmsford Race Committee had received a letter:-

'A movement is on to introduce the game of golf in this district and I have been requested to apply to you to know whether there would be any objection on the part of the Race Committee to the players, at convenient times, making use of the racecourse with other parts of the common provided no damage was done'.

The letter noted that the common was suitable for laying out a nine-hole course and the holes themselves could be placed where they would not interfere with the racecourse although the golfers would play across it. The prospective golfers also asked for the use of a room or rooms in the grandstand. Rather

In 1893 the Race Committee allowed golfers to use part of the Galleywood course.

surprisingly the committee approved the request, without any suggestion of payment, 'provided there is no play on race days'. Although generally the new sports clubs catered for the middle classes, there were also a number of sports and social clubs associated with the newly opened factories. These attracted large memberships and their sports days were prestigious occasions. In 1898, for example, the annual sports meeting of the Crompton Parkinson Chelmsford Arc Works Club attracted a large attendance including the President of the Institution of Electrical Engineers and the Mayor and Mayoress of Chelmsford. It included foot races, cycle races and a tug of war and, in an echo of earlier patronage of horse racing at Galleywood, one prize was awarded by the tradesmen of Chelmsford.

There is evidence that some of these new sports bodies took on, in microcosm, a function very similar to that performed by Chelmsford Races. An account of a meeting of the Executive Committee of the Essex County Cycling Club in 1893 is strikingly reminiscent of accounts of social functions associated with horse racing a century earlier. The report describes how the members of the committee were taken for a drive in a four in hand coach provided by the honorary secretary, Mr Robert Cook, before arriving at his home. Mr Cook's behaviour mirrors that of the race stewards a hundred years before and the wording of the article echoes many reports in the earlier era:- 'All the expenses of the excursion were defrayed by Mr Cook, and upon arrival at White House Farm [his home] the visitors were most hospitably entertained at a sumptuous repast'. The committee then settled down to a meeting presided over by the mayor.

This expansion of spectator as well as participation sports continued into the twentieth century and by the 1930s speedway in particular was booming. There was a track at Rayleigh near

Southend as well as several others within easy reach on the outskirts of London. Billiards and darts among smaller-scale amateur indoor games also grew in the 1930s. In 1932 proposals were put forward for an Essex County Billiards Association and an Essex Amateur Championship was announced at the Palace Hotel in Southend. Darts was also a popular past time with darts leagues usually based on pub teams. In 1936 the area finals of a *News of the World* competition were held at the Golden Fleece in Chelmsford and were reported to have attracted great interest. It is clear that by the 1930s there were many other sporting events available in and around Chelmsford to draw spectators away from Galleywood race meetings and further diminish their importance to the town.

The changing attitudes to sport over the nineteenth and early twentieth centuries were summed up in 1931 by the Rev. Herbert Dunnico who was preaching a sermon at a sportsmen's and sportswomen's service in Colchester. Dunnico was a Labour MP as well as deputy speaker of the Commons and vice-president of the Essex County Football Association. There was a time, he said, when Christian people looked askance and with suspicion upon sport but the Christian Church today was realising that between real healthy sport and religion there was a close bond - that man was made to play just as he was made to pray.

New Pastimes

By the end of the nineteenth century the citizens of Chelmsford had the choice of many outlets for their leisure interests which were not dependent on the existence of the races. In 1880 Chelmsford Museum held a number of scientific meetings with talks on such subjects as 'Darby's Patent Pedestrian Digger', 'Edison's Talking Telephones' and 'Animals With More Than Two Eyes'. It also promoted the Cambridge extra-mural lectures which helped bring more women into higher education.

The Essex Review of 1892 lists a number of societies then in existence, including the Chelmsford Musical Society, The Chelmsford Association of Church Choirs, the Chelmsford Philharmonic Society, the Chelmsford Pianoforte and Vocal Clubs and the 'Private Society for the Practice of Strict Glee and Part-Song Music.' In 1886 the Chelmsford Town Band performed for two hours outside the Shire Hall and a newspaper report suggests this type of entertainment attracted the town's elite who would once have patronised the cultural events surrounding the horse racing. It noted that a further seven concerts had been arranged at the homes of prominent citizens around the town. One of these, for example, was William Duffield. He was a distinguished local solicitor and Liberal politician and, coincidentally, a member of the Chelmsford Race Committee whose family could trace its connections with the area back to the time of Henry VIII.

The range of leisure activities available in this period is further exemplified by those listed in just one 1887 edition of the *Essex Chronicle* (as the *Chelmsford Chronicle* had by then become). These included a performance of a new version of 'Aladdin' at the Corn Exchange by a professional company fresh from a season in Eastbourne (two weeks later a play direct from the Haymarket in

London was also to begin a short season); a meeting of the Old Friars Debating Society and a 'Music and Talk' evening featuring a local vicar and a number of amateur musicians. Chelmsford Cricket Club was also planning a 'smoking evening' the following week.

These organisations had a strong middle class base, however there is also evidence of growing provision of cultural pursuits for the working classes. The same 1887 edition of the Essex Chronicle also lists a meeting of the British Workman Mutual Improvement Society which heard a talk entitled 'The Divine Right of Queens' and a meeting of the Chelmsford Literary and Mechanics Institute. There were also two nights of lectures on 'Socialism' in the town as well as a meeting of the Conservative Working Men's Club. Entertainment options were significantly extended with the opening of the first cinemas in the town in 1912.

Right. An early twentieth century cinema blockbuster! Advertisement from the Essex Chronicle.

OXO
CINEMA FILM
Entitled
"Life on the Oxo Cattle Farms"

Beautiful living pictures of some of the 350,000 OXO cattle – a grand march past of one of the herd – counting cattle – a novice opening of a gate on horseback – a cowboy breaking-in horse – branding calves – a parable of pedigree Hereford OXO Bulls worth £1,000 each – great bulls weighing over a ton plunging into a bath – cowboys separating big bulls from a herd and galloping across the plains. This film will form part of an excellent programme.

SHOWING
THIS WEEK
At
The Picture House,
New Writtle St., Chelmsford

Part II
Racing Returns
to Chelmsford

A False Start

The history of Chelmsford Races might have ended in the dark days of the 1930s had it not been for a local entrepreneur and former show jumper, John Holmes. In 1997 he bought the Essex Showground at Great Leighs, five miles to the north of Chelmsford.

The annual Essex Show, which was run by the Essex Agricultural Society, itself, had a long history with the first show dating back to 1869. The Agricultural Society was formed ten years earlier with a number of founding members also connected to the racing at Galleywood. In 1958 the Essex Show found a permanent home at Great Leighs.

The village magazine noted of that first show:- 'The weather was wet, the ground was muddy and the crowds cheerful'. Until then the village had been something of a rural backwater. In 1949 the local magazine declared:- 'The time has come, and more than come, when water should be laid on to every cottage, also electric power and light.

THE CASTLE
(FORMERLY THE ST.ANNES CASTLE)

The Hermitage/Pilgrim Route.

Pilgrims, day and night, requested a place to lay their heads for the night and a bite to eat together with spiritual comfort. Some were joyfully going to Canterbury from the shrines at Bury and Walsingham, while others were returning with uplifting tales of miracles and magnificent majesty.

Stagecoach Era.

The heavy vehicles connecting London and Norwich ran a daily service in the 18th century. They would have swung through our village carrying as many as could sit or hang on top as well as the passengers inside, complete with luggage. Horses were changed every 10 miles and St. Annes Castle fitted this conveniently between Chelmsford and Braintree.

Once the coach had left the Toll Gate at Little Leighs it would have struggled to get up the hill from the bridge, as the heavy load on a road no more than a dust trap in summer and a mud bath in winter could overturn quite easily.

Once it had arrived, and the passengers alighted and welcomed by the landlord, the stable boys released the horses and fed them, and if necessary bedded them down for the night. The blacksmith, and there were a number in the village, was soon there to check the horses and advise on fresh ones. Then the wheelwright would check the coach and make good any part of it broken or battered by road wear. It was a busy time for our artisans.

Others who benefitted from the coach stop were the locals of all ages, they would crowd into the bar to hear news from Chelmsford and far off London, both places most had never seen. These were always grand tales of highwaymen, fashions and good living and oh such wonderful tales to embellish and spread around to the family and workmates.

St Anne's Castle plaque

Drainage by sewers is a bigger problem, but for householders in a row of council houses on the Main Road to have to dispose of their sewage by individually digging holes is too antiquated for this year of grace ….'

Six years later nine houses in the village were told they could expect to wait another year before getting electricity and as late as 1957 the local magazine reported the village school still didn't have proper water-borne sanitation and urged residents to keeping 'pegging away' to get it installed.

Until the arrival of the Essex Show, Great Leighs' chief claim to fame was as the home of the St Anne's Castle. It is said to be the oldest licensed public house in England. In medieval times it was a hermitage and developed into an inn to provide a resting place for pilgrims on their way to the shrine of Thomas a Becket in Canterbury.

During the latter part of the twentieth century the village was plagued by increasing traffic on the main road. By the 1990s most villagers agreed that something had to be done. An Essex County Council report in 1994 concluded heavy traffic was causing congestion and delay and the accident rate was unacceptably high. However, it was not until 2002 that a dual-carriage bypass was opened, having taken 20 months to build at a cost of £22 million. Not everyone welcomed the new road:- a number of farmers lost land, it cut through part of the Essex Showground and it effectively isolated the tiny village of Little Leighs.

After acquiring the showground John Holmes organised the Essex Show himself until it ended permanently in 2000. He then set about an ambitious project to build an all-weather racetrack on the site – Britain's first new racecourse since the opening of Taunton in 1927. A mile-long, £30 million, all-weather complex was built and opened in the spring of 2008 with good quality racing returning to Chelmsford for the first time in more than 70 years. The venue was very popular with horsemen and one of the features of the new course was an enormous grandstand, transported from the K Club in Ireland where it was used for the 2006 Ryder Cup. It was more than 160 yards long and two storeys high (see opposite). However, with the world recession at its peak, the development ran into problems and in January 2009 the course was placed into administration. Its racing licence was revoked by the British Horseracing Authority which led to closure soon afterwards.

Several rescue deals were discussed including one with George Walker the former boxer and chairman of Brent Walker who built the Brent cross shopping centre in London. But they all came to nothing and for a time it looked as if the site might be redeveloped for another use entirely.

The short lived temporary grandstand on the new course. Opened in 2008 and closed in 2009.

Up and Running Again – Racing Comes Full Circle

Despite the closure of the Great Leighs course in 2009 and the uncertainty over its future, the dream of a return to horse racing in Chelmsford was still alive. Finally, a syndicate headed by Fred Done, owner of the Betfred bookmaking chain, came to the rescue and the track was re-born as Chelmsford City Racecourse. A multi-million-pound renovation included a new £6.5 million grandstand as well as other major work. The new company, Great Leighs Estates Limited, spent £200,000 upgrading the all-weather track and also extended it to create a new seven furlong start. The course re-opened in January 2015 and in its first year held nearly 60 meetings with prize money totalling almost three-and-a-half million pounds. While Galleywood races struggled to meet the £300 a day prize money demanded by the Jockey Club in the late nineteenth century (about £26,000 in today's terms) the average at a Chelmsford City meeting is well over £50,000.

Prize money at this level was only briefly ever seen at Galleywood during the heyday of racing in the 1860s. On occasions prize money for an individual race at Chelmsford City has exceeded £50,000 and the record for a single meeting is £190,000. Since opening, a further half-a-million pounds has been spent in improvements to the course – one of only four floodlit courses in the country.

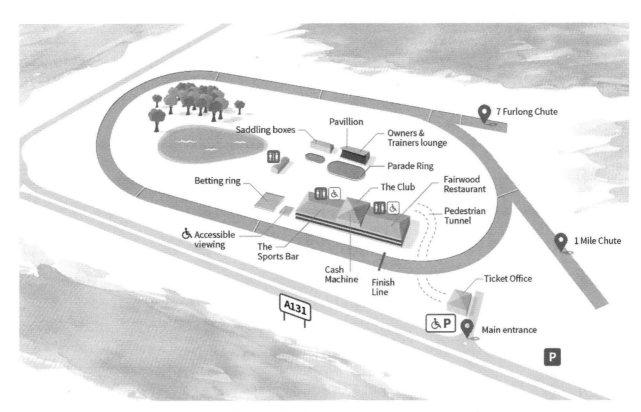

The layout of Chelmsford City Racecourse at Great Leighs

For the future, plans have been approved for a casino inside a new, bigger, grandstand. Plans are also in place for a turf track alongside the all-weather surface.

Just as the coming of the railway in 1842 opened up racing at Galleywood to a wider audience so television in the twenty first century has made racing at Chelmsford City Racecourse accessible not only to a national audience but also to viewers around the world through international picture distribution and on-line streaming. All racing is televised on the satellite/cable channel At the Races and is shown in betting shops around the country. Channel 4 television has also shown meetings.

(Left) Racecard introduction January 11th 2015 – the day racing resumed at Chelmsford City Racecourse in Great Leighs.

This means that horse racing in Chelmsford can now be watched by far more people than at any time in its long history. The media contracts have, in turn, allowed the course to offer high prize money which attracts high class horses and world-class jockeys and trainers. Trainers such as Sir Michael Stoute, John Gosden and Saeed Bin Suroor have all saddled horses at Chelmsford.

Among the jockeys Frankie Dettori, Ryan Moore – who in 2016 was ranked number one in the world – and William Buick have ridden there. Top class horses have included Covert Love who won her first race at Chelmsford in 2015 and later won the Irish Oaks, becoming one of the best fillies in Europe. Buratino became one of the highest rated two-year olds in Europe in 2015 and won at Chelmsford on his first run. Tryster won Chelmsford City's very first race in January 2015 and became the champion all-weather horse of 2015.

It is not only the horse racing that brings echoes of the great days of Galleywood. Chelmsford City Racecourse also hosts large social events and concerts in another reminder of centuries past. June 2015 saw a post-racing concert by Madness which attracted 9,000 people and in the summer of 2016 Simply Red played to a crowd of 9,500. Other events have included Countryside Days, Charity Days and Ladies Days while the grandstand has hosted boxing, comedy and murder mystery nights. Although not yet on the same grand scale, these social occasions resonate back down the years to the carnival days on Galleywood Common.

In April 2016 Chelmsford City staged a first in the history of British horse racing by taking over at 24 hours' notice a meeting which was cancelled at Newbury because of bad weather. That day Chelmsford staged its first 'Group' races – the world-recognised top category of racing – and among the winners was the Queen's horse Dartmouth ridden by Ryan Moore.

Leading jockeys at the new Chelmsford City course: Frankie Dettori (right) and Ryan Moore, who in 2016 was rated the world's top jockey

Buratino ridden by Joe Fanning won on his debut at Chelmsford City in 2015. He went on to become one of the top three highest rated two-year-olds in Europe that year

Panoramic shot of the new grandstand and the track at Chelmsford City from the commentator's box

In addition to thoroughbred racing the course also stages Arabian horse racing fixtures as well as pony and trotting races. In line with most modern racecourses, the facilities at Chelmsford are utilised to a maximum on non-race days with the grandstand regularly used for seminars, conferences, trade fairs, wedding receptions and even training for the emergency services.

FULL CIRCLE

In 2015 Chelmsford City Racecourse provided a tangible link with racing at Galleywood almost a century earlier. The 6.15pm race on March 26th - Len Lefebve's Chelmsford Hat-Trick 91st Anniversary Stakes – commemorated 91 years to the day since Len Lefebve rode three winners in an afternoon at Galleywood.

The event was attended by Len's two sons and members of his family. Len Lefebve was born in 1898 and rode around 150 National Hunt winners during his career. On that day at Galleywood in 1924 he was chased home in two races by a younger colleague, Towser Gosden. Towser was the father of John Gosden who in 2012 was British Champion Flat trainer and who, in an extraordinary twist of fate, trained the winner of Len's memorial race.

So, after an eighty year gap and a journey from Galleywood to its new home at Great Leighs, horse racing in Chelmsford can finally be said to have come full circle.

Len Lefebve in action.
In 2015 Chelmsford City Racecourse commemorated his hat-trick of winners at Galleywood in 1924.

The new grandstand and parade ring at Chelmsford City

The Paddock in 2016 with
racegoers keen to see the Queen's horse (centre).

*Around 9,000 people attended the
Madness concert after racing at Chelmsford City Racecourse in July 2015*

The glamour of Ladies Day at the new course in 2016

Racegoers in the new grandstand at Chelmsford City.

*Dartmouth, owned by the Queen and ridden by Ryan Moore, won the
Group 3 John Porter Stakes at Chelmsford in April 2016*

Flat out under the floodlights

About the Author

David Dunford was born in Chelmsford and attended the University of Essex, graduating with a degree in Government in 1972. He joined Essex County Newspapers in Colchester as a reporter and later became an assistant editor.

In 1978 he moved to the BBC in London where he worked in the Radio Newsroom writing news bulletins for all domestic outlets. He also wrote for Yesterday and Today in Parliament as well as writing and broadcasting on finance for radio, television and the BBC World Service. He later became Editor of the BBC General News Service, responsible for providing news and current affairs for BBC English local radio stations and BBC Scotland, Wales and Northern Ireland. He was also a member of a European Broadcasting Union working party on local radio in Europe. In 2003 he was Editor of all BBC local radio and regional television coverage of the second Gulf War.

After taking early retirement from the BBC he became a visiting lecturer in radio journalism at the University of the Arts in London. In 2014 he returned to Essex University to study for an MA in History which he was awarded with distinction. This book grew out of the dissertation written for his MA.

Determined to win at the new Chelmsford City Racecourse

Selected Bibliography

Abdy, Charles, *Epsom Past,* Philmore and Co., Doncaster, 2001.

Beavis, Jim, *The Croydon Races,* Local History Publications, London, 1999.

Bird, T.H*., Admiral Rous and the English Turf 1795 - 1877,* Putnam, London, 1939.

Borsay, Peter, *The English Urban Renaisance:- Culture and Society in The Provincial Town 1600-1770,* Clarendon Press, Oxford, 1989.

Brailsford, Dennis, *British Sport:- A Social History,* The Lutterworth Press, Cambridge, 1992.

Brown, A.F.J. *Essex at Work 1700 – 1815,* Essex County Council, Chelmsford, 1969.

Brown, A.J.F., *Essex People 1750-1900,* Essex County Council, Chelmsford 1972.

Brown, A.J.F., *Prosperity and Poverty:- Rural Essex 1700-1815*, Essex Record Office, Chelmsford, 1996.

Cannadine, David, *The Decline and Fall of the British Aristocracy,* Yale University Press, New Haven and London, 1990.

Chinn, Carl, *Better Betting with a Decent Feller:- Betting and the British Working Class 1750 – 1990,* Harvester Wheatsheaf, London, 1990.

Coller, D.W., *The People's History of Essex,* Meggs and Chalk, Chelmsford, 1861.

Davidoff L. and Hall C., *Family Fortunes:- Men and Women of the English Middle Class 1780-1850,* Routledge, London, 1987.

Defoe, Daniel, *Tour Through the Eastern Counties,* East Anglian Magazine Ltd, Ipswich, 1949.

Dewar, George A.B., ed, *Memoirs of Sir Claude Champion de Crespigny Bart,* Lawrence and Bullen, London, 1896.

Downes, D.M.,et al, *Gambling, Work and Leisure:- A Study Across Three Areas,* Routledge and Keegan Paul, London, 1976.

Foreman, Stephen, Hylands:- *The Story of an Essex Country House and its Owners,* Ian Henry Publications, Romford 1990.

Grieve, Hilda, *The Sleepers and the Shadows Chelmsford:-* a town its people and its past', vol 2, *From Market Town to Chartered Borough 1608-1888.* Essex Record Office, Chelmsford, 1994.

Harrison, J.F.C., *Late Victorian Britain 1875-1901,* Routledge, London, 1991.

Harvey, Adrian*, The Beginnings of a Commercial Sporting Culture in Britain 1793 -1850*, Ashgate. Aldershot, 2004.

Hawkins, Ted, *Galleywood Racecourse,* Galleywood Historical Society, 2008.

Horn, Pamela, *Pleasures and Pastimes in Victorian Britain,* Sutton Publishing, Stroud, 1999.

Huggins, Mike, *The Victorians and Sport,* Hambledon and London, London, 2004.

Huggins, Mike, *Flat Racing and British Society 1790 – 1914:- A Social and Economic History*, Frank Cass, London, 2000.

Huggins, Mike, Horse *Racing and The British 1919-39,* Manchester University Press, Manchester, 2003.

J.V. Beckett, J.V., *The Aristocracy in England 1660-1914,* Basil Blackwell, Oxford, 1986.

Jones, David, *Chelmsford:-* A History, Phillimore, Chichester, 2003.

Jones, Stephen G., *Workers at Play:- A Social and Economic History of Leisure 1918-1939.*

Johnson, Terry, *Hidden Heritage:- discovering ancient Essex,* Capall Bann Publishing, Chievely, 1996.

Longrigg, Roger, *The History of Horse Racing,* Stein and Day, New York, 1972.

Lutring, Cheryl R., *Lewes Racecourse:- A Legacy Lost?* Phreestyle Pholios, Alfriston, 2013.

Malcolmson, Robert W., *Popular Recreations in English Society 1700 -1850,* Cambridge University Press, Cambridge, 1973.

Marriage, John, *Changing Chelmsford,* Philmore and Co, Chichester, 1992.

McKibben, Ross, *Classes and Cultures:- England 1918-1951,* Oxford University Press, Oxford, 1988.

Miers, David, *Regulating Commercial Gambling:- Past, Present and Future*, Oxford University Press, Oxford, 2004.

Mortimer, Roger, *The Jockey Club*, Cassell, London, 1958.

Munting, Roger, *Hedges and Hurdles:- A Social and Economic History of National Hunt Racing,* J.A.Allen, London, 1987.

Pain, Rollo, Why Cartmel?:- *Survival of a Small Racecourse 1856-1998,* Lakeland Health, Kendal, 2001.

Pitt, Chris, *A Long Time Gone,* Portway, Halifax, 2007.

Plumptre, George*, Back Page Racing:- A Century of Newspaper Coverage,* MacDonald/Queen Anne Press, London, 1996.

Rule, John, *Albion's People:- English Society 1714-1815,* Longman, Harlow, 1992.

Sanders, Muriel, *Glimpses of Galleywood,* Galleywood Parish Council, 1993.

Scott, Marvin B., *The Racing Game,* Aldine Pub. Co., Chicago 1968.

Seth-Smith, Michael (Ed.), *The History of Flat Racing,* New English Library, London, 1978.

Torrey, Gilbert, *Chelmsford Through the Ages,* Ipswich, East Anglian Magazine Ltd, 1977.

Tranter, Neil, *Sport, Economy and Society in Britain 1750-1914,* Cambridge University Press, Cambridge, 1998.

Tyrrel, John, Running Racing:- *The Jockey Club Years Since 1750,* Quiller, London, 1997.

Vamplew, Wray, *Pay Up and Play the Game:- Professional Sport in Britain 1875-1914,* Cambridge University Press, Cambridge, 1988.

Vamplew, Wray, *The Turf:- A Social and Economic History of Horseracing,* Allen Lane, London, 1976.

Walvin, James*, Leisure and Society 1830-1950*, Longman, London, 1978.

Watkinson, Pat, *A Century of Memories,* Leighs Publications, Great Leighs, 2000.

Articles

Bargheer, Stephan, 'The Fools of the Leisure Classes:- Honor, Ridicule and Emergence of Animal Protection Legislation in England, 1740 -1840', *European Journal of Sociology*, vol 47, no 1, 2006.

Crump, Jeremy, 'The Great Carnival of the Year':- The Leicester Races in the 19th Century, *Transactions of the Leicestershire Archaeological and Historical Society*, 58, 1984, 58-74.

Giroud, Mark, 'Victorian Values and the Upper Classes,' *Proceedings of the British Academy*, vol 78, 1992.

Huggins, Mike, 'Culture, Class and Respectability:- Racing and the Middle Classes in the Nineteenth Century', *International Journal of the History of Sport,* vol 11, no1, 1994.

Huggins, Mike, 'Nineteenth Century Racehorse Stables in their Rural Setting:- a Social and Economic Study,' *Rural History*, vol 7, no 2 1996

Pinfold, John, 'Horse Racing and the Upper Classes in the Nineteenth Century,' *Sport in History*, Vol 28, no 3, 2008.

Also available from Essex Hundred Publications

The Essex Hundred
The history of the county of Essex described in 100 poems
and supported with historical notes and illustrations.
A unique book written by Essex poets covering 2000 years of
county history.
ISBN:- 9780955229503 £7.99

Magna Carta in Essex
Essex barons were at the forefront of those who pushed hard
for the Magna Carta, with Robert Fitzwalter, Lord of Dunmow
appointed their leader. Yet within three months of the charter
being sealed England was at war and Essex racked by conflict.
ISBN 9780993108303 £7.99

London's Metropolitan Essex
Events and Personalities, from Essex in London, which shaped
the nation's history.
ISBN 9780955229558 £12.99

**The Essex Hundred Children's Colouring and Activity
Book**
The Colouring and Activity Book is another title from the
Essex Hundred family aimed at children and part written by
children. The book includes not only Essex information but
pictures to colour in, word searches, puzzles and questions.
ISBN:- 9780955229534 £4.99

They Did Their Duty, Essex Farm, Never Forgotten by
Andrew Summers
A book that tells the story of Essex Farm a First World War
cemetery in Belgium that will forever bear the county name
and its connections to the Essex Regiment.
ISBN 9780955229596 RRP £9.99

AEOLUS, Ruler of the Winds
by Shirley Baker
A whimsical story of sailing adventures around the Essex and
Suffolk coast.
ISBN:- 9780955229589 £7.99

The Numbers Had to Tally
by Kazimierz Szmauz
A World War II Extraordinary Tale of Survival
ISBN:- 9780955229572 RRP £8.99
(digital edition available)

Digital Editions available.

Essex Farm
The Numbers Had to Tally
L33 and other stories from WWI

Essex Hundred Publications.
Books written, designed and printed in Essex.
Available from bookshops, book wholesalers, direct from the publisher
or online www.essex100.com